CDM, THE FUTURE OF FEDERAL CYBERSECURITY

HEARING

BEFORE THE

SUBCOMMITTEE ON CYBERSECURITY AND INFRASTRUCTURE PROTECTION

OF THE

COMMITTEE ON HOMELAND SECURITY
HOUSE OF REPRESENTATIVES

ONE HUNDRED FIFTEENTH CONGRESS

SECOND SESSION

JANUARY 17, 2018

Serial No. 115–44

Printed for the use of the Committee on Homeland Security

Available via the World Wide Web: http://www.govinfo.gov

U.S. GOVERNMENT PUBLISHING OFFICE

30–190 PDF   WASHINGTON : 2018

CONTENTS

Page

CDM, THE FUTURE OF FEDERAL CYBERSECURITY

Wednesday, January 17, 2018

U.S. HOUSE OF REPRESENTATIVES,
COMMITTEE ON HOMELAND SECURITY,
SUBCOMMITTEE ON CYBERSECURITY AND
INFRASTRUCTURE PROTECTION,
Washington, DC.

The subcommittee met, pursuant to notice, at 2:09 p.m., in room HVC–210, Capitol Visitor Center, Hon. John Ratcliffe (Chairman of the subcommittee) presiding.

Present: Representatives Ratcliffe, Gallagher, Bacon, Fitzpatrick, Katko, Richmond, Thompson, Demings, Langevin, and Jackson Lee.

Also present: Representative Thompson.

Mr. RATCLIFFE. Good afternoon. The Committee on Homeland Security Subcommittee on Cybersecurity and Infrastructure Protection will come to order.

The subcommittee is meeting today to receive testimony regarding the implementation and future of DHS's Continuous Diagnostics and Mitigation, or CDM, program. I now recognize myself for an opening statement.

In providing effective cybersecurity, the ability of the Federal enterprise to monitor and assess the vulnerabilities and threats to its networks and systems in real time or as near real time as possible is paramount. This is what the Continuous Diagnostics and Mitigation, or CDM, program at DHS is all about, understanding what and who is on Federal networks so that we can achieve true visibility into the Federal Government's digital ecosystem.

Phase 1 of CDM is to provide visibility into Federal networks and information systems by working to identify what was on Federal networks. It was a simple question, really. What hardware and software was on the systems an agency or department was running? This was about taking stock of those internet-connected assets. As DHS has moved through Phase 1, they found an incredible amount of devices connected to our networks that agencies were not previously aware of.

How can you protect what you cannot see? How can you modernize your technology if you do not even know what technology you have? It is no secret that the Government has trouble buying technology. Old and outdated technology is not only a barrier to the Federal Government completing its mission to serve the American people in a digital world, but brings with it insecurities and raises serious cybersecurity risks for each and every agency and department.

DHS began Phase 1 in 2012. While I understand that setting up new Government programs, buying new and advanced technologies, and deploying those technologies across a massive Federal environment is not easy, the threats to Federal agencies, however, continue to grow every minute. The maturity of the Continuous Diagnostics and Mitigation program has to move at the pace of new technologies and innovations, not at the pace of bureaucracy.

To most effectively carry out oversight, we must educate ourselves. While DHS is working with 70-plus Federal agencies and departments from the 24 CFO Act, agencies down to dozens of smaller bureaus and offices, this committee must work to better understand the pace at which cybersecurity technologies are advancing and how programs like CDM are working to protect the dot-gov.

Does DHS have access to the cybersecurity platforms, technologies, and services necessary to make effective continuous monitoring a reality in 5 years, not in 15 years? We must work with the experts leading these charges in the private sector to find ways for more agile adoption of the tools and services we need to defend our networks and our data.

As we have seen with both the private sector and Government data breaches, the identities and privacies of millions of real Americans are at risk here. The Federal Government must work to protect the data of these citizens, including the employees that work within. That is why we are here today: To learn what we are doing right and to learn what we could be doing better.

To a certain extent, what does success look like? The rapidly-evolving threat landscape of modern information age means that the Government must change its processes to ensure that we are not gathering more data than we can really protect. As we continue this conversation, I look forward to hearing from stakeholders throughout the Federal IT space, including technology companies, DHS, and the Federal agencies that they serve. We begin with the private-sector experts joining us today.

CDM is the ambitious program that I believe if implemented well and over a reasonable time line provides the American people with the kind of Federal cybersecurity defense that they deserve. I want to thank the witnesses for their time and I look forward to their testimony today.

[The statement of Chairman Ratcliffe follows:]

STATEMENT OF CHAIRMAN JOHN RATCLIFFE

JANUARY 17, 2018

In providing effective cybersecurity, the ability of the Federal enterprise to monitor and assess the vulnerabilities and threats to its networks and systems, in real time or as near real time as possible, is paramount.

This is what the Continuous Diagnostics and Mitigation—or CDM—program at DHS is all about. Understanding what and who is on Federal networks so that we can achieve true visibility into the Federal Governments' digital ecosystem.

Phase One of CDM is to provide visibility into Federal networks and information systems by working to identify what was on Federal networks.

It was a simple question really: What hardware and software was on the systems an agency or department was running? This was about taking stock of those internet-connected assets.

As DHS has moved through Phase One, they found incredible amounts of devices connected to our networks that agencies were not previously aware of.

How can you protect what you can't see?

How can you modernize your technology if you don't even know what technology you have?

It is no secret that the Government has trouble buying technology.

Old and outdated technology is not only a barrier to the Federal Government completing its mission to serve the American people in a digital world—but brings with it insecurities and raises serious cybersecurity risks for each and every agency and department.

DHS began Phase One in 2012, while I understand that setting up new Government programs, buying new and advanced technologies, and deploying those technologies across a massive Federal environment is not easy, the threats to Federal agencies continue to grow every minute.

The maturity of the Continuing Diagnostics and Mitigation Program has to move at the pace of new technologies and innovations, not at the pace of bureaucracy.

To most effectively carryout oversight, we must educate ourselves. While DHS is working with 70-plus Federal agencies and departments—from the 24 CFO Act agencies down to the dozens of smaller bureaus and offices—this committee must work to better understand the pace at which cybersecurity technologies are advancing and how programs like CDM are working to protect .gov.

Does DHS have access to the cybersecurity platforms, technologies, and services necessary to make effective continuous monitoring a reality—in 5 years not 15 years?

We must work with the experts leading these charges in the private sector to find ways for more agile adoption of the tools and services we need to defend our networks and data.

As we have seen with both private-sector and Government data breaches, the identities and privacy of millions of real Americans are at risk. The Federal Government must work to protect the data of these citizens, including the employees that work within.

That is why we are here today. To learn what we are doing right and what we could be doing better.

And—to a certain extent—what success looks like.

The rapidly-evolving threat landscape of the modern information age means that Government must change its processes to ensure that we aren't gathering more data than we can protect.

As we continue this conversation I look forward to hearing from stakeholders throughout the Federal IT space, including technology companies, DHS and the Federal agencies that they serve.

We begin with the private-sector experts joining us today.

CDM is an ambitious program that I believe, if implemented well and over a reasonable time line, provides the American people the kind of Federal cybersecurity that they deserve.

I want to thank the witnesses for their time and I look forward to their testimony.

Mr. RATCLIFFE. I now recognize the Ranking Minority Member, Mr. Richmond, for any opening statement that he might have.

Mr. RICHMOND. Good afternoon, and thank you to Chairman Ratcliffe for today's hearing on the Department of Homeland Security's Continuous Diagnostics and Mitigation program, CDM.

Today, DHS is working to protect Federal networks by administering two signature programs, Einstein and CDM. These programs work in tandem to keep out unauthorized traffic and provide on-going monitoring and mitigation of cybersecurity risk. Through CDM, the Department works with Federal agencies to procure cybersecurity tools and services to empower them to fend off cyber attacks.

As initially envisioned, CDM will provide each agency with the information and tools necessary to protect its network by, among other things, identifying the assets on the agency's network that warrant protection, bolstering access controls to various elements of an agency's network, and improving situational awareness about activities on an agency's network.

Implementation of CDM, however, has been slower than DHS originally anticipated. Challenges inherent to the size and scope of the task for accounting for all assets on the Federal network, confusion about whether DHS or a customer agency was responsible for footing the bill for CDM-related expenses, and technology gaps in the commercial off-the-shelf markets have collectively slowed the process.

That said, today about 20 agencies have their internal dashboards up and running, two agencies have connected to the Federal dashboard, and by next month, DHS expects that all 24 of its target agencies to be connected to the Federal dashboard. As more agencies connect to the Federal dashboard, DHS will have greater visibility across Federal networks and will be better positioned to identify and mitigate malicious activity, including complex coordinated attacks.

As representatives of vendors who work directly with DHS on CDM, the witnesses here today have a unique perspective on how to ensure Federal agencies continue to prioritize cybersecurity investments, how the Federal Government can implement the lessons learned over the past 5 years to improve the program, and whether contracting personnel have the training necessary to deploy CDM quickly.

I also hope the witnesses can speak to how the Department's failure to name a permanent under secretary for the National Protection and Programs Directorate, along with on-going chief information officer vacancies across the Federal Government, are affecting the implementation of CDM.

Our adversaries have made their interest in breaching Federal networks crystal clear. Just last week, Trend Micro reported that Fancy Bear, the same Russian-backed hacking group that breached the Democratic National Committee in 2016, has been targeting the Senate's network. Although Congressional networks do not participate in CDM, this troubling report serves as a reminder that the interest in breaching U.S. Government networks persists and that the Federal Government must act more quickly to protect itself.

On a final note, this subcommittee is also responsible for ensuring that Federal policies support private-sector efforts to secure critical infrastructure. Last summer, reports emerged that hackers successfully penetrated domestic energy companies and nuclear power plants. In light of the growing cyber threats across critical infrastructure, I will be interested in learning whether the private sector can benefit from implementing elements of CDM, like the dashboard, and whether efforts to implement CDM-like programs are already under way.

I look forward to the insight of our panelists today and I thank you all for being here. With that, Mr. Chairman, I yield back the balance of my time.

[The statement of Ranking Member Richmond follows:]

STATEMENT OF RANKING MEMBER CEDRIC L. RICHMOND

JANUARY 17, 2018

Today, DHS is working to protect Federal networks by administering two signature programs—EINSTEIN and CDM. These programs work in tandem to keep out unauthorized traffic and provide on-going monitoring and mitigation of cybersecurity risks. Through CDM, the Department works with Federal agencies to procure cybersecurity tools and services to empower them to fend off cyber attacks.

As initially envisioned, CDM would provide each agency with the information and tools necessary to protect its network by, among other things, identifying the assets on an agency's network that warrant protection, bolstering access controls to various elements of an agency's network, and improving situational awareness about activities on an agency's network.

Implementation of CDM, however, has been slower than DHS anticipated. Challenges inherent to the size and scope of the task of accounting for all assets on the Federal network, confusion about whether DHS or a customer agency was responsible for footing the bill for CDM-related expenses, and technology gaps in the commercial-off-the-shelf markets have collectively slowed the process.

That said, today about 20 agencies have their internal dashboards up and running and two agencies have connected to the Federal dashboard. And by next month, DHS expects that all 24 of its target agencies to be connected to the Federal dashboard.

As more agencies connect to the Federal dashboard, DHS will have greater visibility across Federal networks and will be better-positioned to identify and mitigate malicious activity, including complex, coordinated attacks.

As representatives of vendors who work directly with DHS on CDM, the witnesses here today have a unique perspective on how to ensure Federal agencies continue to prioritize cybersecurity investments, how the Federal Government can implement the lessons learned over the past 5 years to improve the program, and whether contracting personnel have the training necessary to deploy CDM quickly.

I also hope to witnesses can speak to how the Department's failure to name a permanent under secretary for the National Protection and Programs Directorate, along with on-going chief information officer vacancies across the Federal Government, are affecting implementation of CDM.

Our adversaries have made their interest in breaching Federal networks clear. Just last week, Trend Micro reported that Fancy Bear, the same Russian-backed hacking group that breached the Democratic National Committee in 2016, has been targeting the Senate's network.

Although Congressional networks do not participate in CDM, this troubling report serves as a reminder that the interest in breaching U.S. Government networks persists and that the Federal Government must act more quickly to protect itself.

On a final note, this subcommittee is also responsible for ensuring that Federal policies support private-sector efforts to secure critical infrastructure. Last summer, reports emerged that hackers successfully penetrated domestic energy companies and nuclear power plants.

In light of the growing cyber threats against critical infrastructure, I will be interested in learning whether the private sector can benefit from implementing elements of CDM and whether efforts to implement CDM-like programs are already under way.

Mr. RATCLIFFE. Thank the gentleman. The Chair now recognizes the Ranking Minority Member of the full committee, the gentleman from Mississippi, Mr. Thompson, for an opening statement.

Mr. THOMPSON. Thank you very much, Mr. Chairman and Ranking Member. I want to thank both of you for your on-going work to assess and improve the Department of Homeland Security's efforts to secure Federal networks.

Over the past decade, hackers have breached networks across the Federal Government, including the State Department, the Department of Commerce, the Department of Justice, Department of Energy, and the Office of Personnel Management. These hackers show no sign of slowing down. Instead, their tactics are growing more aggressive and more sophisticated.

Congress has charged the Department of Homeland Security with important responsibilities associated with taking on evolving threats to Federal networks. Chief among these responsibilities is helping Federal agencies improve visibility of network assets and prioritize efforts to correct vulnerabilities. Initiated in August 2013 and formally authorized in 2014, the Continuous Diagnostics and

Mitigation program, commonly called CDM, is supposed to do just that.

Through four phases of implementation, CDM will help agencies understand, No. 1; what assets are on that network; No. 2, who is on their network; No. 3, what is happening on their networks; and, No. 4, how to protect data on their networks. Unfortunately, despite the security benefits CDM can provide, implementation has been slow.

As of last month, nearly 5 years after CDM was launched, only 8 Federal agencies had transitioned to operation and management of Phase 1. A number of reasons have been offered to explain why CDM implementation lagged behind expectations, including ambitious programmatic goals, challenges in reconciling diverse agency structure and architecture, and resource and leadership challenges, among others. The Ranking Member of the subcommittee just talked about the fact that top people are not in place to provide some of the absolute necessity for direction.

There are a number of other things, Mr. Chair, that I could talk about, but I look forward to the testimony and ultimately an opportunity to ask some questions. I yield back.

[The statement of Ranking Member Thompson follows:]

STATEMENT OF RANKING MEMBER BENNIE G. THOMPSON

JANUARY 17, 2018

Over the past decade, hackers have breached networks across the Federal Government, including the State Department, the Department of Commerce, the Department of Justice, the Department of Energy, and the Office of Personnel Management.

These hackers show no signs of slowing down. Instead, their tactics are growing more aggressive and more sophisticated.

Congress has charged the Department of Homeland Security with important responsibilities associated with taking on evolving threats to Federal networks.

Chief among these responsibilities is helping Federal agencies improve visibility of networked assets and prioritize efforts to correct vulnerabilities. Initiated in August 2013 and formally authorized in the 2014, the Continuous Diagnostics and Mitigation Program (CDM) is supposed to do just that.

Through four phases of implementation, CDM will help agencies understand: (1) What assets are on their networks; (2) Who is on their networks; (3) What is happening on their networks; and (4) How to protect data on their networks.

Unfortunately, despite the security benefits CDM can provide, implementation has been slow. As of last month—nearly 5 years after CDM was launched—only 8 Federal agencies had transitioned to operations and management of Phase 1.

A number of reasons have been offered to explain why CDM implementation lagged behind expectations, including ambitious programmatic goals, challenges in reconciling diverse agency structures and architectures, and resource and leadership challenges, among other things.

Indeed, so many explanations for slow CDM implementation have been offered that it is hard to suggest a silver bullet solution. What is clear, however, is that the threats to our Federal networks are far outpacing agency implementation of CDM.

Is critical that we understand why implementation has been so slow so we can give the Department the resources, support, and authority it needs to resolve ongoing implementation challenges.

That is why the expertise of the panelists today is so valuable.

I will be interested in understanding what you all view as the lessons learned from the implementation of Phase 1 that can be applied to improve future implementation of the program.

Mr. RATCLIFFE. Thank the gentleman. Other Members of the committee are reminded that opening statements may be submitted for the record.

[The statement of Hon. Jackson Lee follows:]

STATEMENT OF HONORABLE SHEILA JACKSON LEE

JANUARY 17, 2018

Chairman John Ratcliffe and Ranking Member Cedric Richmond, thank you for today's hearing on "CDM: The Future of Federal Cybersecurity."

This hearing will provide Members of the Committee on Homeland Security with the opportunity to learn more about the Continuous Diagnostics and Mitigation (CDM) program, a key component of the Department of Homeland Security's (DHS) overall effort to protect Federal network.

The Continuous Diagnostics and Mitigation program is an active approach to fortifying the cybersecurity of Government networks and systems.

The task of installing CDM across the Federal Government was too large a task for one contractor so DHS divided the work among several contractors and subcontractors.

Our witnesses will provide valuable insight in the process of installing of CDM throughout the Federal Government:

WITNESSES

- Dan Carayiannis, Federal director, RSA;
- Gregg Mossburg, senior vice president, Federal Strategic Operations Group, CGI;
- Frank Dimina, associate vice president, Federal Civilian Sales, Splunk; and
- Mr. A.R. "Trey" Hodgkins, III, senior vice president, Public Sector, Information Technology Alliance for Public Sector (Democratic Witness).

The security of Federal agency networks has been a major concern of mine since I chaired Subcommittee on Transportation Security, which at that time had jurisdiction over cybersecurity issues.

Earlier this month, the House passed H.R. 3202, the Cyber Vulnerabilities Disclosure Act, which I introduced to address the need for effective and aggressive action to deal with the threat of Zero Day Events.

H.R. 3202 requires the Secretary of Homeland Security to submit a report on the policies and procedures developed for coordinating cyber vulnerability disclosures.

The Continuous Diagnostics and Mitigation or CDM provides Federal departments and agencies with the tools needed to identify cybersecurity risks on an ongoing basis, prioritize these risks based upon potential impacts, and enable cybersecurity personnel to mitigate the most significant problems first.

The Congress established the CDM program to provide adequate, risk-based, and cost-effective cybersecurity and more efficiently allocate cybersecurity resources.

It is true that each Federal agency is responsible for protecting its own information systems; however, some agencies, including DHS, play a larger role in Federal network security.

Under the Federal Information Security Modernization Act, DHS is required to deploy technologies to continuously diagnose or mitigate cyber threats and vulnerabilities and make such capabilities available to agencies upon request.

The law essentially codified the CDM program, which DHS is implementing.

DHS entered into partnership with GSA in 2013 to meet the statutory obligation of the Federal Information Security Modernization Act, which facilitated agencies' purchase of consistent, compliant technologies that offered "Information Security Continuous Monitoring Mitigation" (ISCM).

The first contract was awarded on August 12, 2013, to 17 companies, supported by 20 subcontractors, that received awards under a $6 billion, 5-year companion Continuous-Monitoring-as-a-Service to deliver diagnostic sensors, tools, and dashboards to agencies.

CDM is an essential part of the Department of Homeland Security's overall effort to protect the civilian Federal network.

Implementation of CDM is being phased in under the process established by DHS using several contractors and subcontractors.

There have been a number of challenges to the process of implementing a Federal-wide CDM program.

DHS encountered a number of unexpected challenges during the rollout of Phase 1.

For example, neither DHS nor the customer agencies anticipated how difficult it would be to identify all the hardware and software assets associated to a network and grossly underestimated the number of agency-connected devices, which delayed the purchase and installation of the necessary sensors.

In May 2016, GAO reported that most of the 18 agencies covered by the CFO Act that had high-impact systems were in the early stages of CDM implementation, and many were proceeding with plans to develop their own continuous monitoring-strategies, independent of CDM.

Further, only 2 of the 17 agencies reported that they had completed installation of agency and bureau or component-level dashboards and monitored attributes of authorized users operating in their agency's computing environment.

Due to these unexpected challenges the early estimates of completing Phase 3 by 2017 were not met.

These issues as well as the urgency of protecting Federal agency networks makes it imperative that we have DHS before the committee to provide an update on the CDM program.

I look forward to hearing the testimony from today's witnesses.

Mr. Chairman, I yield back.

Mr. RATCLIFFE. We are pleased to have a distinguished panel of witnesses before us today on this very important topic.

Mr. Frank Dimina is the area vice president for Federal at Splunk. Mr. Dimina's entire 20-year career has been within the cybersecurity industry, including several years as a security operations center director and consultant, providing advisory services and incident response support to public sector and commercial organizations. Thanks for being here.

Mr. Dan Carayiannis is the public sector director for RSA Archer. I noticed in your bio nearly 30 years of IT management and security experience, and I look forward to having the benefit of your insights on that today. I know the full committee does, as well.

Mr. Gregg Mossburg is the senior vice president for strategic operations at CGI Federal. Mr. Mossburg served as a commissioner on the Tech America Foundation 2011 commission on the leadership opportunity in U.S. deployment of the cloud, or cloud 2.0. Migrating to more shared service is certainly an important aspect of the CDM program, and so we are grateful to have you as a witness here today.

Finally, Mr. A.R. "Trey" Hodgkins is the senior vice president for the public sector at the Information Technology Alliance for Public Sector. I saw, Mr. Hodgkins, that you received some awards for your work in IT procurement reform. That experience is one that I think will be very relevant to today's conversation.

I would now like to ask each of you witnesses to stand and raise your right hand so I can swear you in to testify.

[Witnesses sworn.]

Mr. RATCLIFFE. Please let the record reflect that each of the witnesses has been sworn and answered in the affirmative. You may be seated.

The witnesses' full written statements will appear in the record. The Chair now recognizes Mr. Dimina for 5 minutes for his opening statement.

STATEMENT OF FRANK DIMINA, AREA VICE PRESIDENT, FEDERAL, SPLUNK

Mr. DIMINA. Chairman Ratcliffe, Ranking Member Richmond, and Members of the subcommittee, thank you for the opportunity to appear today to discuss the Continuous Diagnostics and Mitigation program at the Department of Homeland Security. My name is Frank Dimina, and I am area vice president of Federal for Splunk.

In this role I have worked with Federal agencies, including DHS, on multiple cybersecurity and data analytics projects. My entire 20-year career has been within the cybersecurity industry, including several years as a security operations center director.

Splunk is a fast-growing software company in San Francisco with a similar mission: Make machine data accessible, usable, and valuable to everyone.

More than 13,000 companies, Government agencies, universities, and other organizations are using the Splunk software. In the cybersecurity arena, Splunk's software platform often serves as the nerve center of an organization's security operation center.

In my testimony today, I will provide my views on three main topics: The progress to date of the CDM program; opportunities to modernize and enhance the CDM program; and supporting CDM's continued success.

The CDM program has made significant progress over the last several years in providing Federal agencies with capabilities that identify cybersecurity risks on an on-going basis, prioritize those risks based on potential impacts, and enable cybersecurity personnel to mitigate the most significant threats first. That progress is due to the dedication and hard work of the CDM team at DHS and the support that this program has received from Congress and DHS leadership.

Phase 1 of CDM, which is focused on determining what is on the network, has helped Federal agencies to identify endpoints on their networks and raise awareness of the extent of their cyber footprint. After deploying Phase 1 tools, some Federal agencies found a significant number of additional endpoints within their enterprise. As a result, those agencies are now carrying out efforts to bring those endpoints into the program.

Phase 2, which focuses on determining who is on the network, is just now rolling into production. DHS and the General Services Administration, or GSA, are in the process of procuring CDM phase 3 and 4, which focuses on determining what is happening on the network. Once fully implemented, phases 3 and 4 will give Federal agencies the ability to move from legacy, time-based system accreditation to dynamic, risk-based, and event-driven authorization. This will vastly improve the overall security posture of the Federal civilian government.

Building on the progress to date, I believe there are important opportunities to further modernize and enhance the CDM program. One key opportunity is to better leverage the existing data collected throughout CDM. In our view, DHS should transform the existing CDM integration layer into a common data analytics fabric that is standardized across the program. The data analytics fabric would serve as a platform for collecting security-relevant data across Federal agencies at scale, while enabling DHS to perform flexible search queries, build robust visualizations, and provide real-time reporting of the results.

There are several key benefits to this approach. First, a common data analytics fabric would improve the granularity of data available to Federal cyber analysts. Today, CDM data presented in the

Federal dashboard is summary data. Like a photograph, summary data provides a snapshot in time, but lacks the fidelity of a live video feed. Providing DHS analysts with greater detail and drill-down capability would significantly enhance their ability to protect the homeland.

Second, this would provide DHS and security teams across Federal agencies with access to data at machine speed. Across Government, there is a clear need for real-time access to cyber data from the analyst up to the executive.

Third, a common data analytics fabric would provide the foundation to correlate CDM data with security data from other shared service initiatives like Einstein. Allowing the analysts at DHS to connect information from Einstein and CDM would be a mission enabler and provide a level of visibility that is not possible today. This approach might also result in additional economic benefits for the Government by standardizing CDM components, reducing human capital expenditures, and enabling operational efficiencies across CDM.

Promoting CDM's continued success over the next several years will require continued funding through appropriations, robust oversight by Congress, and sustained leadership from DHS. Success also requires a smart acquisition strategy that is flexible and encourages participation by innovative cybersecurity companies.

Thoughtful design of the next phase of CDM could help DHS future-proof the program. CDM must allow for additions of new technologies that enable risk-based monitoring and protection for emerging information technology, such as the internet of things, cloud, and micro-services.

In closing, I will reiterate that the CDM program has made important strides. Now is the time to look at modernizing the approach and enhancing the capabilities of this program.

Thank you again for the opportunity to testify before you today. I look forward to answering your questions.

[The prepared statement of Mr. Dimina follows:]

PREPARED STATEMENT OF FRANK DIMINA

JANUARY 17, 2018

Chairman Ratcliffe, Ranking Member Richmond, and Members of the subcommittee: Thank you for the opportunity to appear before the subcommittee to discuss the Continuous Diagnostics and Mitigation (CDM) program at the Department of Homeland Security (DHS).

My name is Frank Dimina, and I serve as the area vice president, Federal for Splunk Inc. In this role, I oversee Splunk's Federal civilian government business. I originally joined Splunk as the director of the homeland security and law enforcement team. During my tenure at Splunk, I have worked with Federal agencies, including DHS, on multiple cybersecurity and data analytics projects. My entire 20-year career has been within the cybersecurity industry, including several years as a Security Operations Center director and as a cybersecurity consultant providing advisory services and incident response support to public sector and commercial organizations.

Splunk is a fast-growing software company based in San Francisco with a singular mission: Make machine data accessible, usable, and valuable to everyone. Machine data is produced by every digital device, including computers, mobile devices, networks, sensors, software applications, and many other sources. Machine data contains valuable information that is used for security, anti-fraud, IT operations, compliance, business analytics, internet of things (IoT), and other use cases. More than 13,000 companies, Government agencies, universities, and other organizations are using the Splunk software platform. In the cybersecurity area, Splunk's software platform often serves as the nerve center of an organization's security operation center, providing a single pane of glass view for security analysts across an organization's entire security posture. Many Federal agencies, including DHS, currently use Splunk.

Before I proceed with the rest of my testimony, I would like to recognize this subcommittee's leadership on the issue of cybersecurity. Cybersecurity is a rapidly-changing landscape, with threat actors and technology providers evolving daily. Legislation and robust Congressional oversight will be critical as we all work in partnership to strengthen cybersecurity on a national, State, local, enterprise, and consumer level.

In my testimony today, I will provide my views on three main topics:
- The progress to date of the CDM program;
- Opportunities to modernize and enhance the CDM program; and
- Supporting CDM's continued success over the next several years.

PROGRESS OF THE CDM PROGRAM

The CDM program, which was established by Congress to provide risk-based and cost-effective cybersecurity across the Federal Government, has made significant progress over the last several years. Through the CDM program, DHS has taken significant steps to provide Federal agencies with capabilities and technologies that identify cybersecurity risks on an on-going basis, prioritize those risks based on potential impacts, and enable cybersecurity personnel to mitigate the most significant threats first.

This progress is due to the dedication and hard work of the CDM team at DHS and the support that the program has received from Congress and DHS leadership. CDM has raised the bar for security and provides a solid foundation for achieving a baseline of protection across the Federal IT landscape.

Members of the Splunk team have been involved with CDM from the very beginning of the program. Currently, Splunk software is deployed as a part of the CDM program at all 24 civilian CFO Act agencies. We have witnessed both the early challenges and the more recent steady and consistent implementation of CDM across Federal agencies. Since the beginning, Splunk has worked with various system integrators supporting the CDM program. That viewpoint has given us unique insights into the operational challenges, successes, and needs of the program.

A critical decision made during the genesis of the CDM program was the adoption of a phased approach. Phase 1 of CDM, which is focused on determining what is on the network, has helped Federal agencies to identify the endpoints on their networks and raise awareness of the extent of their cyber footprint. After deploying phase 1 tools, some Federal agencies found a significant number of additional endpoints within their enterprise. As a result, those agencies are now carrying out efforts to bring those endpoints into the program.

Phase 2, which focuses on determining who is on the network, is just now rolling into production. We believe the goal of phase 2, building a master user record for users of Federal networks, will be essential to threat mitigation and risk awareness across the Federal Government.

DHS and the General Services Administration (GSA) are in the process of procuring CDM phase 3 and phase 4, which focus on determining what is happening on the network, via the Dynamic and Evolving Federal Enterprise Network Defense (DEFEND) Task Order series. Once fully implemented, phases 3 and 4 will give Federal agencies the ability to move from legacy, time-based system accreditation to dynamic, risk-based, and event-driven authorization. This will vastly improve the security posture of the Federal cyber landscape.

MODERNIZING AND ENHANCING CDM

Building on the progress to date, I believe that there are important opportunities to further modernize and enhance the CDM program. One key opportunity is to better leverage the existing data collected throughout CDM.

In our view, DHS should enhance the existing CDM integration layer so it becomes a common data analytics fabric that is standardized across the program. The data analytics fabric would serve as a platform for collecting security-relevant data across Federal agencies at scale, which would enable DHS to perform flexible search queries, build robust visualizations, and provide real-time reporting of the results. There are several key benefits to this approach.

First, a common data analytics fabric would improve the granularity of data available to Federal cyber analysts. Today, CDM data presented in the Federal dashboard is summary data. Like a photograph, summary data provides a snapshot in time, but lacks the fidelity of a live video feed. Providing DHS analysts with greater detail and drill-down capability would significantly enhance their ability to proactively hunt for malicious activity.

Second, a common data analytics fabric would provide DHS and security teams at Federal agencies with drill-down access to granular data at machine speed. Across the Government, there is a clear need for real-time access to cyber data from the analyst up to the executive. Moving this access to machine speed will strengthen the effectiveness of the Government's response to attacks against Federal systems.

Third, a common data analytics fabric would provide the foundation to integrate CDM data with security data from other shared service initiatives like EINSTEIN, the DHS program that provides perimeter defense for Federal agencies. Allowing the analysts at DHS to correlate EINSTEIN and CDM data would be an important step as it would provide a level of visibility that is not possible today.

The approach I have described would enhance efficiencies in cybersecurity and information sharing within DHS and between DHS and agency partners. It might also result in additional economic benefits for the Federal Government by standardizing CDM components, reducing human capital expenditures, and enabling operational efficiencies across CDM.

SUPPORTING CDM'S CONTINUED SUCCESS OVER THE NEXT SEVERAL YEARS

Promoting CDM's continued success over the next several years will require continued funding through appropriations, robust oversight by Congress, and sustained leadership from DHS.

Success also requires a smart acquisition strategy that is flexible and encourages participation by innovative cybersecurity companies. One positive step is the decision by DHS and GSA to move to the GSA Special Item Number (SIN), reflecting lessons learned from the procurements associated with the CDM Blanket Purchase Agreement (BPA). This change instills a flexible approach that allows for CDM technical capabilities to evolve through the Request For Services (RFS) model. We believe the continued adoption of this acquisition strategy will help to keep CDM agile, innovative, and competitive.

Thoughtful design of the next phase of CDM will help DHS to better position the program for the future. CDM must be able to evolve quickly and allow for additions of new technologies that can enable risk-based monitoring and protection for modern practices such as cloud and micro-services.

The future of the CDM program has critical implications for the security and resilience of the Federal Government's infrastructure. CDM can also set a positive example for large organizations outside of the Government, since some of the key concepts of the CDM program have applicability in the private sector.

CONCLUSION

In closing, I will reiterate that the CDM program has made important strides. Now is the time to look at modernizing the approach and enhancing the capabilities of this program.

We look forward to our continued role in the Government-industry partnership that will move CDM forward to the next level.

Thank you for the opportunity to testify before you today. I look forward to answering any questions you might have.

Mr. RATCLIFFE. Thank you, Mr. Dimina.

The Chair now recognizes Mr. Carayiannis for 5 minutes for his opening statement.

STATEMENT OF DAN CARAYIANNIS, PUBLIC SECTOR DIRECTOR, RSA ARCHER

Mr. CARAYIANNIS. Chairman Ratcliffe, Ranking Member Richmond, Ranking Member Thompson, committee, thank you very much for the opportunity to testify today on the Department of Homeland Security's Continuous Diagnostics and Mitigation program. I commend the committee's initiative to better understand this mission-critical program.

My name is Dan Carayiannis, and I have spent over 30 years in the information technology industry. Currently, I am the RSA Archer public sector global director for RSA security, part of Dell

Technologies. I also lead the RSA Archer CDM dashboard program and Archer's initiatives in the Federal, State, local, and the international public sector.

RSA has been in the cybersecurity industry and a leader in that industry for over 30 years, serving more than 14,000 global customers and many sectors of the economy. RSA solutions help detect, investigate, and respond to advanced attacks. We confirm and manage identities. We ultimately reduce intellectual property theft, fraud, and cyber crime.

What is Archer as it relates to CDM today? RSA Archer is the commercial off-the-shelf software solution chosen for the CDM dashboard. The platform is approximately 1,400 global deployments, including many Fortune 100 companies, as well as Government entities. Archer is a flexible, browser-based, scalable, easily deployed, and fully integrated within a comprehensive dashboard architecture meeting DHS's current and future dashboard requirements.

RSA is committed to the continued success of CDM. We meet regularly with key stakeholders within the DHS itself, prime contractors to ensure our technology is well aligned with current and anticipated needs of the program. We have provided flexible licensing arrangements and have undertaken several leases of our products and enhancements that map directly to DHS requirements. We are supporting the CDM program through the dashboard contractor and again also through the various prime contractors.

As a result of our experience and involvement with DHS and the CDM program, we would like to propose the following recommendations. First, we strongly encourage DHS to maintain on-going control of the dashboard. We see the DHS dashboard as both a strategic executive risk management visualization tool as well as an agency operational tool. Standardization and consistently across the Government is critical to programs' success. Having a standardized risk management approach with one organization, DHS, responsible for managing cybersecurity risk across the civilian Government is key and a reason we believe that the program is succeeding and will succeed. Centralized management and standardized risk scoring provides confidence and consistent measurement and representation of risk across all Government departments and agencies.

Second, we encourage DHS to continue facilitating a shared vision approach for program success. Continued dialog among DHS, RSA, and dashboard end-group prime contractors allows us to reflect on our base software and the architecture and its design and plan for future software enhancements to benefit the program going forward.

Third, we encourage an active, on-going training program as part of the DHS initiative. The contractors who have invested in RSA Archer training have accelerated their learning curve on Archer and increased their deployment successes. We also recommend DHS personnel participate in Archer training so they can better understand how they can get more benefit out of the RSA Archer platform as it relates to CDM.

Fourth, we urge the subcommittee to continue its current and strong support of the CDM program and ensure DHS has the necessary authorization and funding to build upon the current implementation.

Finally, we encourage CDM information be analyzed for Government benefits beyond the initial CDM scope. One of the byproduct benefits of CDM and the program that it is serving is the agencies can leverage data aggregated across the Government that are currently out of scope requirements. For example, agencies can enhance their assessment and authorization, or continuity of operations capabilities and processes, by leveraging existing CDM data. Both data elements can be leveraged by agencies to enhance their security posture, their capabilities, and their reactions to threats.

In closing, we believe the CDM program is having a very positive impact on how Government, as well as commercial organizations, think about managing cyber risk. RSA believes the CDM program is well-positioned to help the Federal Government better understand and react to cyber threats. Thank you very much for the opportunity to testify today. I would be happy to answer any questions you may have.

[The prepared statement of Mr. Carayiannis follows:]

PREPARED STATEMENT OF DAN CARAYIANNIS

JANUARY 17, 2018

INTRODUCTION

Chairman Ratcliffe, Ranking Member Richmond, and Members of the committee, thank you for the opportunity to testify today on the Department of Homeland Security (DHS) Continuous Diagnostics and Mitigation (CDM) program. I applaud the committee's efforts to improve cybersecurity across the Federal Government and commend the committee's initiative to better understand this mission-critical program.

My name is Dan Carayiannis and I am the RSA Archer global public sector director for RSA Security, part of Dell Technologies. I have been part of the RSA Archer business unit for 10 years and I'm the RSA lead for the DHS CDM Dashboard. I also lead Archer's initiatives in the Federal, State, local, and international public sector. I have spent over 30 years in the information technology industry.

RSA has been a cyber industry leader for more than 30 years. The more than 14,000 global customers we serve represent many sectors of the economy. Our business helps enable those we work with to effectively detect, investigate, and respond to advanced attacks; confirm and manage identities; and ultimately reduce intellectual property theft, fraud, and cyber crime.

Today, I want to explain how RSA Archer is designed and deployed, how it helps DHS drive greater cybersecurity, and our CDM program recommendations.

ABOUT RSA ARCHER

RSA Archer is a commercial off-the-shelf technology platform that allows organizations to manage multiple domains of risk in a configurable, integrated software system. RSA Archer is the software solution the CDM program is using as a basis for both the agency and Federal dashboards. Our platform and solutions support a range of needs to include a flexible data architecture, integration capabilities, reporting and dashboards, analytical functions as well as notification and workflow functionality. These capabilities provide users with the ability to interact, gather information, and manage data beyond merely cataloging records. With RSA Archer, risk and compliance teams can better manage risks, escalate issues, streamline processes, and make decisions based on the improved organization of data.

RSA Archer has been a technology solution provider in the Governance, Risk, and Compliance industry since 2000. The platform has approximately 1,400 deployments globally, including many of the Fortune 100 companies and Government entities. RSA Archer is used in a variety of applications and methods, ranging from global, cross-functional programs such as enterprise-level risk management to single function or regional implementations to support defined-use cases.

Risk and security management in today's world must be approached as an integrated business solution for a complex business challenge. The RSA Archer Suite includes multi-disciplinary risk management solutions and use cases that address the most critical domains of business risk. RSA Archer solutions incorporate industry standards to quickly implement the processes to achieve the visibility business and technology leaders need. Our use cases have adopted best-practice standards derived from our extensive customer base and industry standards including NIST 800–53, NIST 800–30, NIST CSF, FISMA, ISO31000, ISO27000, COSO, ISO22301, and more. RSA Archer solutions are also designed with a maturity-driven approach that enables organizations to implement risk management processes over time. Our use case model allows customers to target the organization's most pressing needs by mixing and matching use cases as the business requires.

All RSA Archer solutions are implemented on the RSA Archer platform, allowing an organization to build a consolidated technological approach to managing security, risk, and compliance processes. We understand risk, security, and compliance programs require a flexible, sustainable approach and our technology is designed to be highly configurable and customizable. The RSA Archer platform enables organizations to modify RSA Archer use cases to meet their unique requirements with functionality such as configurable workflows, risk calculations, standard and ad hoc dashboard and reports and flexible technology-agnostic data ingest capabilities. Customers are able to tailor applications to meet their business requirements without the need for extensive coding or development skills all of which is of significant benefit to the DHS CDM program. To meet more advanced needs, customers can leverage RSA Archer APIs and integrate external products to meet unique requirements.

RSA Archer features the following key capabilities:
- An integrated reporting engine and does not require external reporting tools;
- Persona-driven reports and dashboards are built into the solutions, along with the ability to create ad hoc reports and dashboards to meet users' needs;
- User interface designed to satisfy both frequent users (risk/compliance/security teams) and infrequent users (business users/first line of defense);
- Integration capabilities that allow organizations to consolidate data from external systems and range from data import to scheduled data feeds to an API;
- Data ingest capabilities that allow for integrations with external information sources without major code/development efforts to quickly consolidate and map external data to RSA Archer applications;
- Flexible risk-scoring functionality as well as robust workflow and notification capabilities enable customers to automate business process.

RSA ARCHER AND CDM

The Federal Government is challenged with a broad range of continuous monitoring security maturity levels and efforts across a wide range of agencies. To address these challenges, CDM provides a framework that enables consistent and automated compliance monitoring and reporting, helps agencies understand risks and vulnerabilities that could impact the security and operation of their enterprise, and does so in a consolidated and accelerated time frame.

RSA Archer provides the base software solution for CDM that is commercial off-the-shelf technology that's flexible, browser-based, scalable, easily deployed, and can be fully integrated within a comprehensive dashboard architecture to meet DHS's current and future dashboard requirements. The RSA Archer Continuous Monitoring software solution was built to meet the needs of Federal agencies as well as commercial organizations by providing mission-critical capabilities essential to the Continuous Monitoring program. In the case of CDM, the software is being configured and customized to support program requirements by MTV, the dashboard prime contractor under DHS's direction. These essentials are:
- Enabling near-real time visibility into the security posture of targeted devices across the enterprise;
- Managing with a risk-based approach by prioritizing security risk data and focusing on "worst first";
- Maintaining a common operational cyber landscape with aggregation and correlation of data to stay current with latest requirements;
- Having real-time alerting capabilities, and advanced reporting and dashboards at multiple levels of the organization in order to help protect infrastructure across network endpoint such as laptops, desktops computers, and servers;
- Protecting sensitive information such as security configurations and vulnerability information while providing access to the proper individuals to mitigate risks;

- Tracking and reporting compliance across vulnerabilities, configurations, assets, and applications; and
- Leveraging and maximizing existing and new agency infrastructure CDM tools.

The CDM project is segmented into multiple phases and functional areas as the DHS diagram below illustrates.

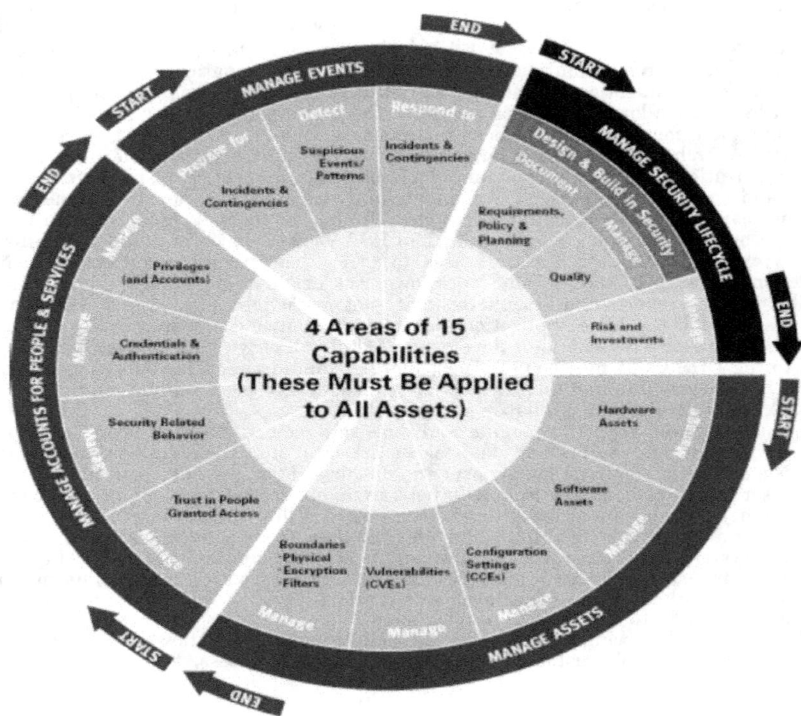

RSA Archer can support the functional areas as outlined by the scope of CDM. The following are examples of how RSA Archer is being used to support the phase 1 CDM functional area:

- *Functional Area—Hardware Asset Manager.*—RSA Archer helps to manage a repository of hardware information assets as a result of its integration with the chosen hardware asset management tool. We are designed to help agencies determine asset classification ratings and required retention periods, determine asset risk, associate the assets with responsible individuals, locations, organizational units, processes they support, facilities where they are housed, and associated with applications they support. RSA Archer can leverage its notification and workflow functionality to support remediation efforts associated with hardware assets and can represent this information in reports, dashboards, and web forms and permit access permissions down to the field level so that multiple levels and views are available to the appropriate organization and personnel for action. In addition, RSA Archer enables agencies to perform on-line assessments to support organization/agency-wide data calls to determine classification ratings and required retention periods.
- *Functional Area—Software Asset Manager.*—RSA Archer helps to manage a repository of software information assets as a result of its integration with your chosen software asset management tool. RSA Archer is designed to help agencies determine asset classification ratings and required retention periods, determine asset risk, associate the assets with responsible individuals, locations, organizational units, processes they support, facilities where they are housed, and associated with applications they support. RSA Archer can leverage its notification and workflow functionality to support remediation efforts associated with software assets and can represent this information in reports, dashboards, and

web forms and permit access permissions down to the field level so that multiple levels and views are available to the appropriate organization and personnel for action. In addition, RSA Archer enables agencies to perform on-line assessments to support organization/agency-wide data calls to determine classification ratings and required retention periods.

- *Functional Area—Configuration Management.*—RSA Archer consolidates data, helps determine asset, application and system risk, and associates configurations with controls, responsible individuals, locations, organizational units, processes they support, and facilities where they are housed. RSA Archer can leverage its notification and workflow functionality to support remediation efforts associated with configuration issues and can represent this information in reports or dashboards. RSA Archer provides an approach for documenting, identifying, managing, and reporting on configuration data at every level of the organization. RSA Archer allows agencies to consolidate controls across multiple regulatory and business requirements into one integrated framework.
- *Functional Area—Vulnerability Management.*—RSA Archer consolidates threat data and reports on threat remediation activities and enables a consistent, repeatable threat management process. RSA Archer consolidates vulnerability, malicious code, and patch information from security intelligence providers, and captures vulnerability results from scan technologies into one threat-management system. RSA Archer then cross-references this information with applications, assets, individuals, and organizational units. RSA Archer leverages its notification and workflow functionality to support remediation efforts associated with vulnerabilities and can represent this information in reports, dashboards, and web forms and permit access permissions down to the field level so that multiple levels and views are available to the appropriate organization and personnel for action.

In summary, RSA Archer is critical in helping DHS realize its goal of comprehensive CDM across the .gov landscape. This includes a hierarchical deployment of agency-level dashboards rolling up summary results to the Federal dashboard. RSA Archer's role is to aggregate summary data collected from various technologies and data stores, calculate and score risk, notify users of changing data, and enable workflow business processes. This aligns specifically with the concepts of RSA Archer as a system of engagement (gathering data and enabling processes) and system of insight (providing aggregated data for decision support).

Additionally, RSA Archer is helping DHS CDM address the many different personas interacting with the "systems of engagement" and "system of insight." A simple way to think of this is to use the concepts of 1st, 2nd, and 3rd Lines of Defense ("LoD"). This concept, referenced in operational risk management strategies, provides a straightforward method to stratify the risk management program and using Archer is being applied by DHS.

In terms of the CDM project, RSA Archer takes the rollup of data from 1st LoD (sensors, endpoints, etc. via a variety of technologies) to inform and drive mitigation activities at the 2nd LoD at the individual agency-level dashboards and facilitating oversight and visibility to the 3rd LoD at the DHS Federal Dashboard level.

CDM IMPLEMENTATION AND RECOMMENDATIONS

RSA is committed to CDM as its commercial software manufacturer and technology partner. We have actively worked with the DHS CDM Project Management Office ("DHS") as the "customer," as well as with the dashboard and prime contractors. We have ensured that our leadership is engaged with project and progress updates, have provided flexible licensing arrangements, and continue to evolve our technology strategy to meet CDM requirements today and anticipate future needs. We meet regularly with key stakeholders within DHS and prime contractors to ensure our technology is aligned to DHS's requirements.

To this end, we have expanded several of our development plans to ensure DHS benefits from the CDM program improvements. DHS, CDM, and Archer are pushing the boundaries on how a large enterprise should think about, manage, and respond to today's security threats as well as prepare for tomorrow's unknowns. This project not only benefits our Nation's security but provides significant private-sector security benefits as well.

To date, we have undertaken and released several product enhancements aligned with DHS's requirements. For example, in the 6.3 version of our platform, released in October 2017, several improvements and architectural changes were made based on feedback from DHS and its contractors to accelerate data ingest processes. We are also working on additional changes to ensure RSA Archer meets its design goal of flexibility and also enhanced performance for data management and calculations which will help DHS make risk-based decisions in near-real time.

We are supporting the CDM program through the dashboard contractor MTV and also through the various prime contractors. This support is being provided through our Technical Support, Services, and Engineering organizations. While we are the software manufacturer, we fully recognize the role and functional elements of the agency level as well as the Federal dashboard and continue to fine-tune our base software solution and platform to accommodate defined and anticipated requirements.

As a result of our experience and involvement with DHS in the CDM program, we propose the following recommendations:

First, we strongly encourage DHS to maintain on-going control of the dashboard.— We see the CDM dashboard as both a strategic executive risk management visualization tool as well as an agency operational tool. Standardization and consistency across the Government is critical to program success and having a standardized risk management approach with one organization, DHS, responsible for managing cybersecurity risk across the civilian government marketspace is a primary reason we believe the program is succeeding. DHS may not be able to respond in a timely fashion without a centralized management approach or if it is being constrained by a distributed agency funding model. Once fully deployed, we believe this highly-controlled approach will render more consistent and accurate metrics across the Government, better cyber risk-based decisions, where necessary faster remediation and encourage standardization and a common consistent measurement and expression of risk across the Federal Government. Regardless of the deployed tools and data stores used, centralized management and standardized risk scoring methodology provides a true "apples-to-apples" comparison from agency-level dashboards to the Federal-level dashboard, giving the Government confidence in consistent measurement and representation of risk.

Second, we encourage DHS to continue facilitating a shared vision approach for program success.—Continued dialog among DHS, RSA, and the dashboard and group prime contractors allows us to reflect on our base software architecture and plan for future software enhancements to benefit the program going forward. We also recommend DHS continue to allow RSA to participate in DHS and its dashboard prime contractor technical exchange meetings on a quarterly or semi-annual basis so we can stay current with anticipated requirements.

Third, we encourage an active, on-going training program as part of the CDM initiative.—The contractors who have invested in RSA Archer training have accelerated their learning curve on Archer and increased their deployment success. As DHS CDM dashboards are fully deployed across the Federal civilian agencies, we believe its critical agency prime contractors have RSA Archer administrators with the skills and experience necessary to maximize dashboard capabilities.

We also recommend DHS personnel participate in RSA Archer training to better understand the RSA Archer platform as it relates to the DHS CDM program and in the future. With the successful rollout of dashboards across all Government agencies, we recommend agency personnel "user" training to maximize the value DHS and the Government are getting out of its dashboard investment such as embedded training videos, on-line training and more.

Fourth, we recommend careful considerations be put in place during the dashboard re-compete process.—We believe the follow-on dashboard prime contract holder should have the necessary RSA Archer skills and capabilities to accept dashboard responsibilities "mid-stream" and continue to manage, configure, and customize the dashboard without issue. Given the learning curve we have seen the dashboard contractor go through to configure and customize RSA Archer to support DHS CDM dashboard requirements, ensuring technical personnel are fully trained and experienced is a prudent and necessary element of continued success.

Fifth, we urge the subcommittee to continue its strong support of the CDM program and ensure it has the necessary authorization and resources for full and expanded implementation.—It is essential DHS has the necessary funding for the on-going phases of CDM to build upon the current implementations and success.

Finally, we encourage CDM information be analyzed for benefits beyond the immediate CDM scope.—One of the bi-product benefits of the DHS CDM program is that agencies can leverage CDM aggregated data to support other "out of scope" agency requirements. For example, agencies can enhance their assessment and authorization and continuity of operations processes by leveraging critical data elements CDM has captured. We believe this saves the Government not only time but also funding.

CONCLUSION

In closing, we believe the CDM program is having a very positive impact on how governments as well as commercial organizations think about managing cyber risk. In today's world, cyber threats are real, coming from multiple vectors, and constantly changing. RSA believes the CDM program is well-positioned to help the Federal Government better understand and react to these cyber threats.

Thank you Chairman Ratcliffe and Ranking Member Richmond and all Members of the subcommittee for your dedication to addressing cybersecurity and to the CDM program. I thank you for the opportunity to be here today and I look forward to working with you and your colleagues in Congress as cybersecurity remains at the forefront of so many policy decisions we face. I'd be happy to answer any questions the subcommittee may have.

Mr. RATCLIFFE. Thank you, Mr. Carayiannis.

The Chair recognizes Mr. Mossburg for 5 minutes.

STATEMENT OF GREGG T. MOSSBURG, SENIOR VICE PRESIDENT FOR STRATEGIC OPERATIONS, CGI FEDERAL

Mr. MOSSBURG. Good afternoon, Chairman Ratcliffe, Ranking Member Richmond, and other distinguished Members of the subcommittee. My name is Gregg Mossburg. I am the senior vice president for strategic operations at CGI Federal.

On behalf of CGI Federal's 6,000-plus dedicated employees providing services to over 100 Federal departments and agencies, I appreciate the opportunity to testify on the progress being made to better secure the Federal Government's systems through Continuous Diagnostics and Mitigation.

CGI Federal plays an important role in the CDM initiative, in providing credential management to users at all 23 CFO Act agencies and three others to enable greater visibility. Providing security to any single network is a challenge. Recognizing the enormity of scaling across the entire Federal environment, DHS is using an incremental approach to identify and deploy capabilities to participating agencies.

The first phase of the CDM program began in January 2013. CDM Phase 1 examined what was on the network. Through discovery tools, a Federal agency can identify all of its hardware and software. Using policies and rules, a determination can be made about whether an asset should be on the network. Next, CDM tools can be used to install patches, continuously scan for vulnerabilities, and ensure software is configured properly and securely.

Studies have shown that cyber hygiene—including asset management, scanning, patching, and proper configuration controls—can stop up to 85 percent of cyber attacks. At the completion of Phase 1, every device in the Federal Government will have a Master Device Record, allowing increased visibility and management.

In June 2016, DHS began rolling out CDM Phase 2, focusing on who is on the network. This phase applies the same concept of cyber hygiene to users, collecting and aggregating information about users from multiple systems into a central location from which agencies are able to monitor different aspects about their network users. This data is important because research continues to show that many security breaches are linked to improper use of credentials, including access through accounts that should have been terminated. Further, this information will permit Federal agencies to verify that only authorized users with the proper credentials are accessing their networks.

Soon, DHS will be rolling out Phases 3 and 4, which focuses on what is happening on the network and how the data itself is protected. Data from all CDM phases is channeled to agency-level dashboards for display and action. Information from these agency dashboards is aggregated into a Federal-level dashboard to provide a Government-wide view of how agencies are performing and identify the greatest areas of risk.

I am especially pleased that the subcommittee has both tools and systems integration represented at the table today. CDM often is discussed in the context of tool acquisition, and yet the integration and consulting services provided are key to Federal agency success, given the shortage of cybersecurity professionals, the vast number of security products available, and competing IT priorities. CDM provides not only cyber expertise, but also training, testing, and governance support.

In structuring the CDM acquisitions, DHS has had the difficult task of balancing the customized solutions for each agency with leveraging economies of scale and solution repeatability. DHS also needed to balance the benefits of using a single integrator with deep solution expertise versus multiple integrators with agency-specific knowledge. As a result, DHS and their contracting partner at GSA, a group known as Fedsim, carefully evaluated and addressed these trade-offs in the new series of CDM acquisitions called Defend. The new Defend strategy provides a variety of benefits that I would be glad to discuss during the Q&A period.

As noted earlier, CGI Federal currently is delivering the credential management solution to 26 agencies under a 2-year task order. To date, this complicated IT implementation effort has enjoyed remarkable collaboration among CGI Federal, the agencies, and DHS, supported by GSA Fedsim. In fact, early deployments already have provided agencies with insight into potential issues that can now be addressed.

While everyone feels the urgency brought on by continuous cyber attacks, it is important to not lose sight of the fact that providing security to networks as large and complex as those of the U.S. Government is an enormous undertaking that requires a solid foundation on which to build advanced capabilities. CDM is one of the first efforts of its type, and we should recognize the impact that it is having.

Let me close first by thanking the folks at DHS and GSA's Fedsim office for their partnership and urgency in supporting the CDM implementation. All are focused on schedules, budgets, and a relentless drive to get the best from industry. I also want to thank the subcommittee for making CDM a priority. Mr. Chairman, I look forward to answering any questions that you or the subcommittee may have. Thank you.

[The prepared statement of Mr. Mossburg follows:]

PREPARED STATEMENT OF GREGG T. MOSSBURG

JANUARY 17, 2018

Good afternoon, Chairman Ratcliffe, Ranking Member Richmond, and other distinguished Members of the Subcommittee on Cybersecurity and Infrastructure Protection. My name is Gregg Mossburg. I am the senior vice president for Strategic Operations for CGI Federal Inc. ("CGI Federal").

CGI Federal, a wholly-owned U.S. operating subsidiary of CGI Group Inc., is dedicated to partnering with Federal agencies to provide solutions for defense, civilian, health care, and intelligence missions. Founded in 1976, CGI Group Inc. is the fifth-largest independent information technology and business process services firm in the world. CGI Group Inc.'s approximately 71,000 professionals serve thousands of global clients from offices and delivery centers around the world, leveraging a comprehensive portfolio of services including high-end business and IT consulting, systems integration, application development and maintenance, and infrastructure management, as well as 150 intellectual property-based services and solutions.

On behalf of CGI Federal's 6,000-plus dedicated employees providing services to over 100 departments and agencies across the Federal Government, I appreciate the opportunity to testify before the subcommittee on the progress being made to better secure the Federal Government's systems through Continuous Diagnostics and Mitigation—otherwise known as CDM.

CGI Federal plays an important role in the CDM initiative, providing credential management ("CREDMGMT") to users at all 23 Chief Financial Officer ("CFO") Act agencies and 3 other agencies to enable greater network visibility. In the next few minutes, I would like to elaborate on the CDM program in general and some of the key factors that have led to very positive collaboration and progress among CGI Federal and its various Federal agency clients.

CDM: RISK-BASED, COST-EFFECTIVE CYBERSECURITY ACROSS THE FEDERAL GOVERNMENT

As you know, cyber threats are growing and evolving continuously. While it is not possible to eliminate or even block all cyber threats, it is critical that the Federal Government and its contractors focus on identifying security risks, allowing leaders to allocate resources where they will have the greatest impact. To this end, Congress established the CDM program to provide risk-based, cost-effective cybersecurity across the Federal Government.

The U.S. Government operates some of the largest and most critical networks in the country. As a result, providing security to any one network is a challenge and scaling across the entire Federal environment is even more daunting. Consequently, DHS is using an incremental CDM approach to identify and deploy capabilities to participating Federal agencies.

THE FOUR-PHASE ROLLOUT

The first phase of the CDM program began in January 2013. CDM Phase 1 examined what is on the network. Through discovery tools, a Federal agency can identify all of its hardware and software. Using policies and rules, a determination can be made about whether an asset should be on the network. If it shouldn't be on the network, then it can be removed. If it should be on the network, then CDM tools can be used to install patches, continuously scan for vulnerabilities, and ensure that software is configured properly and securely.

While it may not sound as glamorous as penetration testing and cyber threat hunting, studies have shown that cyber hygiene, which consists of four essential activities—i.e., effective asset management, scanning, patching, and proper configuration controls—can stop up to 85 percent of cyber attacks. At the completion of Phase 1, every device in the Federal Government will have a Master Device Record, allowing increased visibility into these activities.

In June 2016, DHS began rolling out CDM Phase 2. Phase 2 focuses on who is on the network. This phase applies the same concept of "cyber hygiene" to users and helps measure how well agencies comply with existing Federal mandates such as the Federal Information System Management Act ("FISMA") and the Homeland Security Presidential Directive ("HSPD") 12. The Phase 2 solutions collect and aggregate information about users from multiple systems into a central location from which agencies are able to monitor different aspects about the users on their respective networks. The centralized Master User Record ("MUR") provides information about individual users to include the degree of vetting, training completed, and credentials issued. This data is important because research continues to show that many security breaches are linked to improper use of credentials (including access through accounts that should have been terminated). Not only will the information collected through the CREDMGMT system allow agencies to understand who is on their network, but it will permit Federal agencies to verify that only authorized users with the proper credentials are accessing their networks.

Soon, DHS will be rolling out Phase 3 of the CDM program. Phase 3 is focused on what is happening on the network and looks to protect the network by monitoring traffic across the boundary and performing software code inspection, application weakness detection, development, and supply chain risk management. Phase 3 also seeks to help agencies manage security events by preparing for and responding to security incidents using a new automated risk assessment process to replace the current manual, time-intensive process.

The requirements for CDM Phase 4 are still evolving, but DHS has indicated that it will focus on how data is protected through technologies such as micro-segmentation, digital rights management, and other advanced data protections.

Data from all phases of the CDM program is channeled to agency-level dashboards for display and action. Information from these agency dashboards is aggregated into a Federal-level dashboard to provide a Government-wide view of how agencies are performing and identify the greatest areas of risk for corrective action. This data also can be analyzed and presented in meaningful ways to various consumers and decision makers such as senior leaders interested in trend analysis and technical experts looking to take a deep dive into the detailed technical information.

DEPLOYMENT ACROSS AGENCIES

Not only is DHS incrementally rolling out cyber capabilities, it has taken a staggered approach to deploying those capabilities to all Federal agencies. In Phase 1, agencies were divided into buying groups of 5–7 agencies (Groups A, B, C, D, E, and F) with a single integrator responsible for deploying a solution to agencies in each group, typically over a 3-year period. For Phase 2, DHS issued 2 task orders each with a 2-year duration. The first task order addresses privileged users (i.e., users with extra power or control over the computer system who have the ability to do the most harm) at 65 Federal agencies. This task order effort is commonly referred to as the privilege management (or "PRIVMGMT") task order. The second task order—which CGI Federal currently is delivering—is CREDMGMT, which has a 2-year duration and covers all users at 23 CFO Act and 3 other agencies.

The CDM program often is discussed in the context of tool acquisition. Yet, the integration and consulting services provided are key to Federal agency success. Given the shortage of cybersecurity professionals, the vast number of security products available, and competing IT priorities, Federal agencies often are in need of cybersecurity experts and skilled IT resources. The CDM program recognizes these needs and provides not only cyber expertise, but also services for training, testing, and governance to help agencies develop processes and policies.

A NEW CDM ACQUISITION STRATEGY

As with all programs of this size, there are trade-offs to be considered. For example:
- the economies of scale and repeatability of using a consistent solution across the Federal Government versus tailoring to a specific agency's existing infrastructure and processes;
- using a single integrator with deep expertise in a solution across a large number of agencies may speed overall deployment, but delay agency-specific process changes; and
- a single integrator supporting an agency for a long period of time will have a deep understanding of the agency's environment, but may not have the required expertise in all cyber products.

As a result, DHS and GSA–FEDSIM carefully evaluated these trade-offs with the lessons learned on the original CDM contract and addressed them in the new series of CDM acquisitions, called Dynamic and Evolving Federal Enterprise Network Defense (or "DEFEND").

Some of the benefits of the new DEFEND strategy include:
- Providing a longer period of performance to encourage a strategic partnership between the integrator, agency, and DHS while helping to address the challenge of processing background investigations for multiple integrators;
- Creating a separate acquisition process for tools and implementing a CDM Approved Products List ("APL") to remove the tool vendors' dependency on integrators;
- Providing flexible funding scenarios, such as incremental funding, allowing agencies to jointly fund efforts with DHS, and surge options; and
- Providing agencies at different levels of maturity with the flexibility to address their most pressing needs.

A COLLABORATIVE PARTNERSHIP

As noted earlier, CGI Federal currently is delivering the CREDMGMT solution to 26 agencies under a 2-year task order. To date, this complicated IT implementation effort has enjoyed remarkable collaboration among CGI Federal, the agencies, and

DHS (supported by GSA–FEDSIM), allowing the team to make great progress. In fact, early deployments already have provided agencies with insight into potential issues that now can be addressed.

AN IMPRESSIVE UNDERTAKING

While everyone feels the urgency brought on by continuous cyber attacks, it is important to not lose sight of the fact that providing security to networks as large and complex as those of the U.S. Government is an enormous undertaking. This is one of the first efforts of its type; therefore, it is critical to lay a solid foundation on these programs before building more advanced capabilities.

CGI Federal is proud to support the CDM program and help its Federal agency clients protect our country's networks, assets, and information. CGI Federal relishes this rare opportunity to work across the entire Federal Government to identify trends and connect agencies to share best practices and lessons learned.

Let me close first by thanking the folks at DHS, and particularly the National Protection and Programs Directorate, for their partnership and urgency in supporting the CDM implementation. It would be an understatement to say that DHS is responsible for overcoming numerous critical challenges in the protection of our country every day. CGI Federal respects DHS's focus on schedules, budgets, and its relentless drive to get the best from industry. I also want to thank this subcommittee for its continued oversight to ensure the continued success of the CDM program. Mr. Chairman, I look forward to answering any questions that you or the subcommittee may have.

Mr. RATCLIFFE. Thank you, Mr. Mossburg. Chair now recognizes Mr. Hodgkins for his opening statement.

STATEMENT OF A.R. "TREY" HODGKINS, III, SENIOR VICE PRESIDENT, PUBLIC SECTOR, INFORMATION TECHNOLOGY ALLIANCE FOR PUBLIC SECTOR

Mr. HODGKINS. Thank you, Mr. Chairman, Ranking Member Richmond, and Members of the committee. On behalf of the members of the IT Alliance for Public Sector, or ITAPS, thank you for the opportunity to share our perspectives today on the Department of Homeland Security Continuous Diagnostics and Mitigation program.

ITAPS represents almost 90 of the most innovative companies offering IT goods and services in the Federal public sector. We applaud the committee's efforts to understand and explore the CDM program, the state of CDM tool acquisition, and what barriers and policy or practice exists for rolling out CDM across the Federal Government.

Last year, ITAPS provided the administration with numerous recommendations to modernize Federal cybersecurity practices, including how to protect Federal networks through accelerated adoption of EINSTEIN and the CDM program. These recommendations include requiring regular automated vulnerability scanning of Federal networks, updating procurement guidance to reflect the fleet of cyber threats, expanding existing programs to recruit and retain a strong cybersecurity work force, and leveraging new technology and integrating security tools into IT deployments.

DHS is implementing recommendations included in the President's IT modernization report. These range from securing Government systems and commercial clouds, something not included in the original CDM plan, to completing the acquisition strategy for new long-term task orders that offer CDM life cycle support to agencies. ITAPS suggests that Congress focus on the following.

No. 1, accelerate procurement cycles to keep pace with cyber threats. The committee should work to ensure that there are sufficient numbers of adequately trained contracting personnel to deploy CDM tools in a timely fashion to keep up with the evolving threat landscape.

No. 2, accelerate adoption of CDM through oversight. The committee should exercise oversight to ensure that agencies are prioritizing funding for CDM solutions, because agencies are reluctant to contribute to funding their own security. Many do not put a line item in their budget requests and seek to solely rely upon DHS funding for CDM deployment. Unpredictable Federal appropriations substantially contribute to this condition, as agencies are not able to effectively plan, identify, acquire, and deploy cyber tools in truncated budget cycles.

No. 3, experienced personnel with appropriate skill sets and vendors with proven success at an enterprise scale are critical to the success of CDM. The committee should work with DHS to ensure that the acquisition plan for Phase 3 contemplates the skills necessary for effective implementation, the budget to attract and retain individuals with such skills and vendor qualifications based on experienced success.

No. 4, protect data, protect Federal data. It has been almost 3 years since the OPM data breach, and DHS has yet to implement Phase 4 of CDM, to provide data-level protection capabilities, such as digital rights, management, micro-segmentation, and data masking.

No. 5, enhance accountability for agency adoption and deployment of CDM through robust use of the CDM dashboard. The Federal dashboard compiles summary feeds from all the agencies regarding their adoption and deployment of CDM. This tool will eventually provide a broad view of the Government's cyber posture to help DHS and OMB determine where resources are needed to strengthen agency systems. The CDM dashboard is also one specific means for Congress to hold agencies accountable for their progress.

No. 6, the CDM program office should educate State, local, and Tribal governments about the CDM tools and capabilities available. States, localities, and Tribal governments are facing similar cyber challenges and threats, and governments have made cybersecurity a top priority, but many need help with protecting their data and networks. The committee should work with DHS to create an outreach program to ensure that these other government jurisdictions are aware of CDM, the tools and capabilities that are available, and how they can acquire CDM capabilities for their own use through Schedule 70 at GSA.

No. 7, ensure adequate means to attract and retain a cyber skilled work force. Congress should create innovative means to attract cyber skilled applicants and retain them once hired. It should also look to rapidly draw down the security clearance backlog. Imagine what the Government cyber work force would look like and could do if just 10 percent of the over 700,000 employees and contractors awaiting investigations could get cleared.

To close, Mr. Chairman, the technology sector supports the CDM program and its various phases as an important and effective means to secure the Federal Government networks and systems. More improvements can be made, though, and I hope that our recommendations can help the committee focus on making CDM better. We look forward to the opportunity to work with Congress and the Department on this important issue, and I am happy to answer your questions at the appropriate time.

Thank you.

[The prepared statement of Mr. Hodgkins follows:]

PREPARED STATEMENT OF A.R. "TREY" HODGKINS, III

JANUARY 17, 2018

INTRODUCTION

On behalf of the members of the IT Alliance for Public Sector (ITAPS), we appreciate the opportunity to share our perspectives on the Department of Homeland Security (DHS) Continuous Diagnostics and Mitigation (CDM) program. We applaud the committee's efforts to understand and explore industry perspectives on the CDM program, the state of CDM tool acquisition, and what barriers there are, in policy or practice, to rolling out CDM across the Federal Government to improve cybersecurity across the Federal Government as cyber threats evolve.

Last year, ITAPS, with its members, undertook an effort to provide the Trump administration with numerous recommendations to modernize Federal cybersecurity practices, including how to protect Federal networks through accelerated adoption of EINSTEIN and the CDM program. With the interconnected and global nature of today's digital environment, strong cybersecurity must be a fundamental underpinning of any effort to transform Federal IT systems and is essential to realizing the expected economic and efficiency benefits of IT modernization.

The diversity of recommendations contained in our final report reflects the reality that enhancing cybersecurity requires a comprehensive strategy that leverages people, processes, and technological innovations to actively prevent cyber attacks, and holistically reduce enterprise cybersecurity risks. These recommendations outline actions that can be taken now to enhance the Federal Government's cybersecurity posture, such as requiring regular, automated, vulnerability scanning of all Federal network environments, updating procurement guidance to reflect the speed of cyber threats and the rapid evolution of security technologies, and expanding existing programs to recruit and retain a strong cybersecurity workforce.

Importantly, our report also offers key themes and recommendations focused on taking advantage of new evolutions in technology and natively integrating strong security tools into IT deployments. To succeed in new shared service and cloud-based environments, it is critical for Government to prioritize implementing security technologies that can work together in an automated, holistic way to actively prevent, not just detect, cyber attacks across the entire Federal Government's network infrastructure. To keep up with the pace of modern cyber attacks and reduce risk on an enterprise-wide basis, security tools must be capable of automatic reprogramming based on new threat data to deliver consistent security across the entirety of the network, including all cloud and endpoint environments.

Adopting IT systems with agile security technology that can protect digital infrastructure at scale is vital, because the Federal Government simply cannot continue to divert people and resources toward manually maintaining antiquated systems or manually correlating cybersecurity incidents. Indeed, new, and emerging technology trends—including the increased adoption of cloud, shared services, and virtualized networks—also present critical opportunities to fundamentally simplify and automate how the Government consumes and delivers cybersecurity tools to reduce enterprise risks. The emergence of shared, cloud-based marketplaces where security capabilities can be seamlessly tested and deployed as application-based software—an alternative to time-intensive hardware procurement, evaluation, installation, and system integration cycles—represents the agility the Government must evolve to.

Similarly, there must be a focus on making information sharing as automated and actionable as possible. This means collapsing the amount of time between when an organization receives a technical indicator and the implementation of a preventive control to enforce security based on that threat information. Further, Government and industry must mature information-sharing processes to focus on sharing more than isolated indicators of compromise and incentivize the sharing of correlated threat indicators that link together multiple steps of the adversary's playbook, aligned to each phase of the attack life cycle—including reconnaissance, weaponization, delivery, exploitation, and command-and-control.

Finally, our recommendations offer opportunities for continued public-private partnership. An integrated approach between Government and industry can enhance everyone's collective cybersecurity by fostering a shared understanding of the cyber threat landscape, facilitating a more robust and systemic public-private threat information-sharing environment, jointly developing effective policies, and partnering to raise education, awareness, and overall levels of cybersecurity skills. Private-sector innovation will be critical in replacing legacy Federal IT systems with next-generation solutions that both spur greater efficiencies and strengthen the security of the Nation's digital infrastructure.

For this testimony, we will focus on our CDM recommendations from the report and concerns raised by our members regarding Phase 3 and 4. As you know, the 4-year-old CDM program is delivering capabilities to agencies in four phases: Phase 1 (What is on the Network?), Phase 2 (Who is on the Network?), BOUND (Protecting the boundaries), Phase 3 (What is happening on the Network?) and Phase 4 (Protecting the data on the Network). On May 15, 2017, DHS reported at an industry briefing that 24 major and almost 40 small agencies were engaged in implementing CDM Phases 1 and 2 requirements. DHS is planning for these agencies to transition to operational status by the end of fiscal 2018. The Department is also implementing recommendations included in the President's IT modernization report. These changes range from addressing securing Government systems in commercial clouds—something not included in the original CDM plan—and completing the acquisition strategy for new, long-term task orders to offer CDM life-cycle support to agencies. Finally, they are now providing solution development and implementation for Phases 3 and 4, in addition to future work. DHS and GSA have also added supply chain risk management into the program, requiring vendors to complete a questionnaire to provide DHS information on how their product was manufactured and to help the agency understand the supply chain of the products vendors are offering to be included on the CDM approved products list. We would recommend that Congress focus on the following:

Cybersecurity threats to the U.S. Government are outpacing the Federal acquisition process, creating vulnerabilities. ITAPS has recommended to both the administration and the Congress that the path to increased cybersecurity protections for Government networks is through IT modernization, and that acquisition reform is essential to the ability to modernize IT in the Government and attain greater cyber assurance. In other words, we cannot have cybersecurity without IT modernization, and we cannot acquire the goods and services we need for either of these goals without changing the way we acquire IT. To make progress on this goal, ITAPS makes the following recommendations:

1. Encourage Full Utilization of and Update Government Procurement Rules to Enable Agencies to Compete with Hackers

Current procurement rules in place at various Federal Government agencies preclude them from effectively countering the hacker threat in a timely manner. It is critical that DHS and other Federal agencies have access to the same tools. This can only be achieved by encouraging full use of current procurement rules, and by looking for opportunities to update those rules where necessary. Currently, there are numerous ways Federal agencies can acquire products and services rapidly including:

- Through the Federal Acquisition Streamlining Act of 1994 (FASA), Congress mandated, to the maximum extent practicable, the use of simplified acquisition procedures (SAPs) for products and services not exceeding the simplified acquisition threshold.
- The Competition in Contracting Act of 1984 (CICA) allows Federal agencies to accelerate the acquisition process where there is an urgent need, or where requiring full and open competition could compromise National security.
- The U.S. General Services Administration (GSA) maintains a supply schedule for information technology (Schedule 70), where pre-vetted vendors with pre-negotiated terms offer cybersecurity products.
- Congress authorized the Continuous Diagnostics and Mitigation (CDM) program at DHS, which allows Federal agencies to expand their CDM capabilities through the acquisition of commercial off-the-shelf tools, with robust terms for technical modernization as threats change.
- Congress has granted 11 agencies (including DHS) the ability to enter into "other transaction agreements," which generally do not follow a standard format or include terms and conditions normally found in contracts or grants, in order to meet project requirements and mission needs.

In addition to encouraging Federal agencies to fully use these procedures, procurement policy, and acquisition procedures must evolve more rapidly to match the pace of information technology development and adoption by hackers, criminals, and other bad actors. Currently, little guidance exists in the Federal Acquisition Regulations (FAR) regarding the procurement of cybersecurity technology; rather, the FAR leaves cybersecurity implementation to each individual Federal agency. Agency officials and contractors must consult a myriad of different agency regulations to ascertain if and how other agencies have implemented their acquisition regulations regarding cybersecurity. This diversity in agency cybersecurity regulations undermines security requirements and policies governing Federal procurements. Harmonizing cybersecurity acquisition requirements would allow agencies to: (1) Target security to highest-priority data and threats; (2) obtain greater value through reduced compliance obligations and increased contractor focus on high-value cybersecurity investments; and (3) enhance agency cybersecurity through the adoption of best practices, tempered through public review and comment.

- The Director of the Office of Management and Budget (OMB), in consultation with the administrator of the Office of Federal Procurement Policy (OFPP), as key National priorities should: (1) Provide clear direction to security and acquisition officials across Government that cybersecurity solutions should be acquired and implemented rapidly; (2) advise and train security and acquisition officials on existing authorities available for the rapid acquisition and implementation of cybersecurity solutions; (3) expeditiously identify impediments to the rapid acquisition and implementation of cybersecurity solutions that need to be addressed by Congress and report those impediments to the relevant committees of jurisdiction for redress; and, (4) provide reciprocity of security clearances for cybersecurity professionals to deploy CDM from agency to agency .
- The administration should assess disparate cybersecurity acquisition requirements across agencies and make recommendations to harmonize requirements to the greatest extent possible.

2. Protect Federal Networks through Accelerated Adoption of Einstein and Continuous Diagnostics and Mitigation (CDM)

A significant number of recent Federal breaches resulted from compromised identities, including those of privileged users. The EINSTEIN and Continuous Diagnostics and Mitigation (CDM) programs, when fully deployed,[1] will help Government agencies acquire vital security capabilities and tools to better secure Government networks and systems. The EINSTEIN program is designed to detect and block cyber attacks from compromising Federal agencies, and to use threat information detected in one agency to help other Government agencies and the private sector to protect themselves. The CDM program provides Federal departments and agencies with capabilities and tools that identify cybersecurity risks on an on-going basis, prioritize these risks based upon potential impacts, and enable cybersecurity personnel to mitigate the most significant problems first.

Our primary recommendations in this space are the need for deployment, procurement flexibility, and improvements in the workforce development process. Currently, Federal agencies recognize the value in deploying CDM solutions. They also recognize, however, that these deployments could be paid for by DHS in the following appropriations cycle. Agility and speed are very important in this context. Ultimately, a plan and a strategy are inconsequential without deployment. There is a distinct risk of a moral hazard where agencies will fail to prioritize cyber funding in the short term, thinking that the associated costs will be borne by DHS, as the cybersecurity executive agency, leaving them susceptible to risk of a significant breach in the interim. Further, DHS partners with GSA on the development of contract vehicles for these programs, and there is a need for more trained contracting personnel to accelerate deployment of these new contract vehicles.

Most departments and agencies have already deployed a variety of authentication and authorization solutions as part of both their internal and citizen-facing applications. ITAPS recommends that any Government-wide solution add value and not create disruption and unintended expense by replacing the existing work that has been done. The applications that have been built and secured with these existing Federal Identity, Credential, and Access Management (FICAM) solutions are servicing millions of people today. Agencies should be encouraged and funded to do what is best for meeting their business requirements: Leveraging APIs to further extend their baseline solutions and adding additional safeguards, like privileged account

---

[1] As evidenced by GAO–16–294, *DHS Needs to Enhance Capabilities, Improve Planning, and Support Greater Adoption of Its National Cybersecurity Protection System,* thoughtful deployment has to consider compatibility with newer/modern technology adoption so agencies can reflect a holistic security risk posture while aligning with the administration's IT modernization goals.

and shared account management. Any new policies coming out of this program should consider and augment the investments and the services already being provided, not direct them to new platforms and distract them from the ancillary opportunities.

In the wake of the OPM breach, Government officials worked tirelessly to improve systems. These are committed individuals, and the sense of urgency following the breach resulted in quick and decisive action to resolve significant challenges that became immediately apparent. Long-term success in implementing those decisions, however, may be hamstrung by backlogs in the procurement process. Reacting to specific events to shore up defenses is different than proactive planning. As we look forward, we believe there is opportunity for DHS and its partner agencies to leverage the lessons learned in the cyber sprint and apply them proactively to enhance overall cyber posture across the Federal Government.

3. CDM Capability Deployment: Recommendations based on earlier CDM Phases.

DEFEND/Phase 3 has yet to be delivered as only one Task Order Request (TOR) has been awarded and work has yet to begin. DEFEND is a significant departure from prior iterations having incorporated feedback received from agencies during earlier phases to offer greater choice and increased flexibility.

Due to the heterogeneity of large enterprise environments the technologies to secure, monitor, and maintain an agency's enterprise systems vary widely. Similarly, the ability of many vendor solutions to properly scale to support complex environments and integrate with existing toolsets may be unproven. Issues with the deployment of technologies to address CDM requirements not only impacts the project schedule, but consumes limited agency resources and hinders the overall success of CDM within a given agency.

We recommend that the CDM program should endeavor where possible to recommend solutions that can demonstrate past performance of successful implementations at enterprise scale. Additionally, due to the size and complexity of any given agency, the CDM program should recommend vendor subject-matter experts be incorporated into the procurement of any new CDM tool deployment initiative over a certain size. The inclusion of experienced, trained, and vetted resources will greatly increase the likelihood of a timely, successful implementation with minimal user impact.

The CDM program should also drive real change in cybersecurity. We need a different approach where technology—enabled by strong collaboration—can be deployed rapidly to security platforms so they can communicate with each other over open communication protocols. Organizations in both the public and private sector need security tools that are interoperable and interchangeable to protect against existing and prospective threats. As cybersecurity solutions become interoperable, they become more efficient and cost-effective. They also become easier to maintain than an IT environment of disparate systems. Over time, more interoperable cybersecurity systems will also contribute to closing the skills gap, as these systems become more widely deployed, require less manual intervention and rely upon more consistent skill sets.

Customers deserve the ability to deploy best-of-breed security solutions, but if they need to install a complete infrastructure just to do so, then agencies lose. By having interoperable standards for interface and exchange formats, the industry could move to a more plug-and-play capability for security products. This has been successful in the past with efforts such as the Security Content Automation Protocol (SCAP), currently in use in the Host-Based Security System (HBSS) and CDM programs. SCAP provides a wide variety of vendors the ability to exchange compliance and patch validation content.

We encourage the Government to work with the private sector to make the vision of a truly open and interoperable cybersecurity ecosystem become a reality. Such an ecosystem promotes a great deal of competition and innovation. At the same time, it also promotes collaboration—making sure that systems work together. The real benefit is an environment that promotes enough competition to deliver innovative solutions, coupled with collaboration to ensure that these new and innovative solutions can work together. Much like the railroad industry that agreed on basic rules of the road—e.g., size and gauge of the tracks and right of ways—the security industry needs rules of the road to allow cooperation, so that firms can compete on implementations to allow for as much innovation as possible.

4. DHS must develop a strategy to evolve and extend CDM protections beyond the network to include protecting Federal data and assets.

In the wake of the OPM data breach in June 2015, OMB and DHS reviewed the state of cybersecurity across Government and developed the Cybersecurity Strategy and Implementation Plan (CSIP), the Cybersecurity National Action Plan (CNAP), the revised OMB Circular A–130 and a host of other Federal policies such as the Cybersecurity Act of 2015 aimed at improving our cyber posture. One of the key findings and requirements included in these Federal cyber policies and the fiscal year 2017/fiscal year 2018 DHS Continuous Diagnostics & Mitigation (CDM) budget requests was to evolve the CDM program beyond network security to include data-level protection capabilities (digital rights management, micro-segmentation, data masking, etc.) for 70+ agencies.

- The recent DHS CDM program update (attached) and the fiscal year and fiscal year DHS CDM Congressional budget justifications (attached) states its intention to move to a new Phase 4 of "data level protection capabilities" to "include additional tools and services to protect sensitive and high value assets data" for Federal Government agencies.
- The 2018 White House Federal IT Modernization Report to the President also stresses the importance for Federal agencies with high-value assets and sensitive information to deploy "data-level protection capabilities and shared services within 180 days."

It's been almost 3 years since the OPM data breach and, unfortunately, the Department has yet to provide any data-level protection capabilities via Phase 4 or any other phase of CDM. In light of the numerous data breaches experienced by the Federal Government in recent years, it is critical for DHS to begin implementing CDM Phase 4 as soon as possible, in order to ensure sensitive and high-value information is protected. We are aware that the Department is focusing on full implementation of CDM Phase 2 & 3, but we believe it should be deploying CDM Phase 4 simultaneously, in order to improve our Government's cybersecurity capabilities and protect high-value assets at the data level. We encourage DHS to focus on building awareness with agency CDM leaders on how to get funding and support for rolling out data protection/Phase 4 capabilities.

Considering the current state of the acquisition capabilities of the CDM program and the cyber threat landscape that Federal ".gov" agencies face, we recommend posing the following questions to DHS, GSA, and any other agencies that have identified high-value assets:

- What is your acquisition time line to roll out Phase 4 or "data-level protection" capabilities in fiscal year 2018?
- Have DHS and GSA considered accelerating the adoption of Phase 4 capabilities for all Government agencies? What is delaying the release of Phase 4 task force orders?
- What CDM training is taking place to ensure Federal agency Chief Information Officers (CIOs) and Chief Information Security Officers (CISOs) are prepared to deploy Phase 4 CDM protections?
- How are CIOs and CISOs planning and budgeting to adopt such "data-level protection" capabilities?
- Can agencies that are ahead of the curve utilize CDM program funding to deploy data-level protection capabilities right now?

5. Encourage DHS to continue progress with the CDM Federal dashboard and educate Federal agencies on the use and benefits.

We recommend that DHS continue and expand the use of the CDM Dashboard to help agencies with their vulnerability management. Developing the Dashboard features and values, highlighting those benefits, and providing the values through the Dashboard across the variety of Federal infrastructures is one challenge. The other obvious challenge is to normalize any score or "grade" that the agency receives fair and relevant. Because of the: (1) Variation in network infrastructure, (2) the variety of measurement tools, and (3) the qualitative nature of the scoring, DHS will be challenged to develop a methodology that appears "fair" and delivers actual value to the agencies as well as the entire Federal infrastructure. Historically, FISMA and FITARA scores were honed through time. We expect CDM scoring to take a similar path.

The Federal dashboard will compile summary feeds from all the agency dashboards, which will give the administration a broad view of the Government's cyber posture. Eventually, the Federal dashboard will help DHS and OMB decide where best to direct their resources to strengthen agency systems. The CDM dashboard is one specific area where transparency and public disclosure of agency performance can drive accountability for their progress.

6. DHS and GSA should work with State/local and Tribal governments to educate them on their access to the CDM tools for network monitoring and security through GSA's Schedule 70.

State/local and Tribal governments are facing similar cyber challenges and threats. The Governors have made cybersecurity a top priority, but they need help with protecting their data and networks. Purchasing has not been high by State/local and Tribal governments, so DHS and GSA should conduct an outreach campaign to assist State/local and Tribal governments with using the CDM catalog.

Thank you again for the opportunity to share these thoughts. If you have any questions, please feel free to let me know. We look forward to working with the committee and your colleagues in Congress to improve the cyber posture for Federal networks and the private sector.

Mr. RATCLIFFE. Thank you, Mr. Hodgkins. The Chair now recognizes the gentleman from Wisconsin, Mr. Gallagher, for 5 minutes for questions.

Mr. GALLAGHER. Thank you, Mr. Chairman. Thank you to all the witnesses for taking the time to be with us on this important topic.

It sounds like everyone shares a relatively optimistic assessment of CDM so far. So I would just—to put it in plain terms, given that in Phase 1 we have basically learned how many devices were on Federal networks that Federal agencies did not know about to the sort-of shadow IT phenomenon, which presents a huge problem for all of us, I just—for whoever wants to take the question, do you feel confident that we have a total picture of what is on Federal networks at this point? If not, how long will it take to have total visibility into what devices are connected and connecting to our networks? Do not all jump at once. We can just go—we can go from here that way, yes.

Mr. HODGKINS. I can go first, Gregg. Just share that we do not believe the Government has total visibility into the assets it possesses on its networks and systems. It has done inventories for specific purposes, for example, risk mitigation, but it does not understand everything it owns.

One of the things that we have identified in the procurement process that can help change that is, No. 1, the Government should create the inventory, but, No. 2, it should begin to keep track of the things it is buying and deploying as it buys them. Currently, the systems that are used to acquire these tools, for example, in CDM and any other capability the Government acquires do not inventory those goods and services as they are acquired.

So there is no running track, no running inventory, no automated means of keeping track of what we are buying and what perhaps we are retiring. So we think that would be an area that could be improved, yes.

Mr. GALLAGHER. Sir?

Mr. MOSSBURG. Go down the line in order?

Mr. GALLAGHER. Yes.

Mr. MOSSBURG. So I would echo, I do not think that we have got the complete picture yet of all of the IT assets, but the point is, as—or the goal is, as Phase 1 is completed, that you would get to a point where you had a complete inventory. I think what Trey said is very important. It does not end, right? We are going to keep buying and keep adding to the inventory, and so the process has got to be kept in place and it is got to be an on-going vigilance to achieve that.

The other element I would add is, the scope is—as addressed in Defend, which is the next phase of CDM, has got to expand between on-prem, or on-premises, inventory out into the cloud and mobile devices to make sure that we are really drawing the circle around the right goal, if you will.

Mr. GALLAGHER. Sure, sure.

Mr. CARAYIANNIS. I think that was one of the challenges that the beginning of the program people encountered was a lot of the agencies—there was more there than they thought. I think people had to kind-of step back, understand that, document all that, before they can progress and move forward.

Certainly, if you have all that data of all those assets, all that information and collecting all that, there is a lot of interesting things you could do about that and report on it and track it. Tracking not just an individual asset, but potentially even someday component parts that make up that asset, which will also be important from a cybersecurity threat perspective.

Mr. GALLAGHER. Thank you.

Mr. DIMINA. I agree with everything said so far. I will just add that continuous monitoring should be looked as a journey, not a destination. There has been great success so far, and that visibility is not complete, but there is a solid foundation for cybersecurity program here. That data can provide immense value both from a risk-scoring perspective and for the ability for agencies and DHS to respond to incidents and perform threat analytics.

So I agree with the comments that there is more progress to come, but I think there is a success story here and the foundation has been built.

Mr. GALLAGHER. Sure. Then obviously as that Phase 1 journey continues and evolves, we want to make sure we are making progress on the other phases. Mr. Hodgkins, I think you mentioned something about Phase 4, and I just wonder, could you tell me, how would a delay in implementation of Phase 3 and 4 impact our ability to protect the Federal.gov domain? Besides adequate funding levels, what does the CDM program need to make sure that we are reaching our goals in those subsequent phases?

Mr. HODGKINS. Well, I touched on a number of elements that Congress could perhaps focus on to improve. One is that agencies now are—they seem to be relying on the pool of money that Congress gives to DHS for this activity as a means of funding all of the CDM activities even within the agencies. The inconsistent budget process has also contributed, because agencies cannot begin to spend dollars until they are appropriated. If their planning, their execution, their identification of contractors, identification of which tools they need happens and we end up with a fiscal year where only 5 months are actually appropriated, it is too short of a time frame to effectively complete that, deploy the activity, and get the dollars obligated for a contractor.

So it creates tremendous challenges. Those are some areas that delay the implementation of a lot of programs, including CDM. Delaying CDM in the way that you are talking about Phase 3 and 4 do not get us to the end point that we have all discussed or raised in some form or fashion as fast as we need to get there. The threats are happening now, and we need to move forward. I mentioned accelerating acquisition cycles. There is a variety of ways that we can do that to try and improve that.

Mr. GALLAGHER. Well, I have run out of time, but thank you for raising the budgetary picture. I know we are grappling with that this week, and we tend to talk about it only in the context of hard defense, but it impacts everything the Federal Government does. So, thank you. Thank you, Mr. Chairman.

Mr. RATCLIFFE. Thank the gentleman. The Chair now recognizes the Ranking Member, Mr. Richmond, for his questions.

Mr. RICHMOND. Thank you. I will start with all the witnesses. There is a work force component to CDM, in that agencies need to organize their cybersecurity and other personnel to implement the use of CDM. How is the shortage of skilled cyber professionals throughout the Federal Government impacting CDM performance? In any order?

Mr. HODGKINS. It is actually having a tremendous impact, Mr. Richmond. I noted, for example, that it is a challenge for both the Federal Government and contracting employees to be deployed when they can not get their clearances through that process in an efficient and timely fashion. There are over 700,000 sitting there. Truly, imagine what we could do if we could get just 10 percent of that through and deploy those people for work for the cyber work force.

We also have challenges in that, you know, people come into the Federal Government, they learn skills, and then they move into the private sector. People from the private sector is also a challenge getting them to come back in. There are a number of exercises underway now to try and identify incentives for companies to lend, if you will, their best and brightest to come and work on some of these problems in the Federal Government.

The center of excellence exercise that is going on now through the White House to deploy the IT modernization plan is an example of trying to implement that, where they are seeking to bring in subject-matter expertise from outside to help address and define requirements to solve problems like cybersecurity and then they can execute internally with their own employees and they can also bring in additional contract personnel.

Mr. MOSSBURG. Thank you. Thanks for the question, Congressman. As I noted in my opening remarks, I was very appreciative that this committee had both tool vendors and systems integration at the table. I think that is an important part to consider in addressing the skills gap that you raised.

There is no question that there is a skills challenge in the Federal Government and also in the private sector, and it really is going to take continued collaboration between them both to make sure we have got the necessary skills to implement successfully the CDM program.

Mr. RICHMOND. Well, but you also mentioned in your testimony about the learning curve. I guess my next question would be: Is there a need for more training on how to use CDM capabilities like the dashboard and then, No. 2, do agencies need help developing or updating their internal governance to make sure it is compatible with CDM?

Mr. MOSSBURG. Yes, I think the answer to both questions is yes. The scope of both training and governance is included in the CDM program so that as these technologies are implemented and processes are put in place, that training and governance is part of the individual task orders and agency implementations.

Mr. RICHMOND. OK.

Mr. CARAYIANNIS. Congressman Richmond, as it relates to the dashboard specifically, absolutely there is a need for training to ensure that once it is fully operationalized at the agency level and even at the Federal level that personnel are trained to get the maximum value out of what it is presenting, the risk scores, calculations that are occurring, understanding what threats might be out there. Having to have trained personnel to be able to understand and act on that is critically important. So an on-going training element just around the dashboard itself I would highly recommend, and that was in my opening remarks.

Mr. DIMINA. So I would add to that that—the private sector is dealing with the same problem. The cyber skills shortage is real and across the board, and it is impacting Government, it is impacting private sector. I do think there are opportunities to look at how can we—and that problem would not be solved in the short term. That is going to take a while to solve across the board between industry and Government, and that continued partnership.

I do think there are some things the industry can do from a technology perspective to help offset some of those challenges. There is work on-going in part of the cybersecurity industry in a space called orchestration automation. Those tools are maturing. While that would not solve the problem completely, those can help add efficiencies to the program.

Additionally, what the core of our testimony from Splunk and my testimony today is about is leveraging what has already been invested and leveraging the data that is already present in the CDM system to gain greater efficiencies and to enhance the mission at DHS. Speaking from personal experience in my time working in cyber operations, the data being collected today is being used for risk profiling and for risk prioritization and for visibility, and that is great. That is a core requirement of the security program. But there is an opportunity to also use that data from an operational perspective and to assist in the mission for threat hunting and understanding the tactics and techniques of APTs out there.

So I do believe that is a problem, and I do believe technology can help. It would not completely solve it, but there are ways to improve the productivity of the investments made today.

Mr. RICHMOND. Thank you, and I yield back.

Mr. RATCLIFFE. Thank the gentleman. Chair now recognizes myself for questions.

So following up on your comment earlier, Mr. Dimina, about CDM being a journey, not a destination, and some of the testimony that we have already heard, I mean, I think at Phase 1 not having full visibility, that is understandable. Obviously, we all want it to be rolled out to all four phases more quickly, and I know there is challenges with respect to that. But I guess as we approach sort-of the halftime or intermission of this program, if you will, I guess I want to hear on the record from all of you that once we get to

Phase 4, as fully implemented, do we still foresee CDM as a program that will be effective and agile and nimble enough to deal with the cyber threats that we are facing at that point in time? I will just go across the board.

Mr. DIMINA. So there is a lot to that question. I think—and thank you for the question, sir. I think regarding specifically Phase 4, you know, the requires are not still defined there, so I think there is some work that still needs to be done to figure out what is going to be accomplished, how it is going to be accomplished to offer data protection.

I think the challenge and an issue that needs to be addressed there, is there are major disruptions occurring in the private sector to the way IT is delivered and handled. Traditional IT is being replaced by server-less models, the rise of micro-services and containers and software-defined networking. So as DHS and team and CDM leadership figure out their approach for Phase 4, I think that is an issue and question that will need to be addressed, because where does data reside in a server-less architecture? That is a challenge ahead.

Beyond that, I think looking at continuous monitoring as a program and to answer your question about where does it go, you know, today we have a foundation. You cannot secure what you cannot see. But the vision would be something that is near real time. To Congressman Richmond's point in his opening remarks, providing situational awareness. You could envision a State where we have the equivalent of a cyber weather map, whereas meteorologists today look at atmospheric data to predict weather threats and weather patterns across the country, once we reached that State and we have successful real-time monitoring and being able to access data at a granular level, we could predict from activity occurring in one part of the Government or see warning signs that would happen at other parts.

You know, in a perfect world, and if we take that one step further, you know, we could have the equivalent of a tornado warning, where attacks against one part of the Government are being seen and reacted to in real-time, and then the cyber defenders in our Government can take proactive actions to defend in advance of those attacks.

Mr. CARAYIANNIS. Congressman, I guess a couple thoughts around that. First, I think once we get to Phase 4 and potentially beyond, an opportunity that I think CDM provides is the tuning of it and extracting more value out of it over the course of time, kind-of from moving from more of a cyber hygiene program to more of a highly-tuned response program where I could quickly interact with anything and everything that I have from an information source perspective, be able to leverage that information to react, rather than days and weeks to hours to minutes.

I think one of the challenges that CDM has identified—and you have heard some of the comments about that today—and one of the opportunities that CDM presents is to really orchestrate a highly-defined environment that could accelerate people's time to action and in time to action dealing with a threat that is out there. The threat will continue. It will continue to progress and become more nimble, and so we need to able to do the same thing. I think CDM is a great start to do that. It is tuning that environment and making it more productive over the course of time for all.

Mr. MOSSBURG. Thank you, Congressman, for the question. I will just put a small fine point on this. I think that it truly is a journey, not a destination. I do not think this is something that we need to think about as getting to done. I think this is something that we need to continually improve and remain vigilant on.

I think we ought to strive for a vision that is not even real-time or predictive, but really gets—or, excuse me, not even real-time, but predictive in nature and begins to look at behavioral analytics and some of the activities that can be correlated across the domain or the enterprise to begin to predict where we may run into problems, both internal to an agency and external to an agency. I think that is the vision that we ought to strive for.

Mr. HODGKINS. I would just add, to echo the comments, that CDM will survive if it can evolve. It has got to keep pace with the threats. It has also got to keep pace with the evolution of technology, the innovation of technologies, you know, as was noted, new forms of computing capabilities as they come down the pike.

Then it has also got to—this is not an operation occurring in isolation. The Federal Government is undertaking significant strides to modernize specific networks and systems, and those will begin to incorporate new cybersecurity capabilities that can then be connected with CDM or can share information with CDM in new ways that we cannot do today.

Mr. RATCLIFFE. My time is expired, but I have a question I want to ask, and if you can answer it quickly and if not incorporate some answers into some of the other Members' questions, but, you know, to this theme of CDM being a journey, my question I guess is for all of the folks up here: What is the low-hanging fruit for us as legislators? Where can we work to make effective changes to make the CDM journey faster and better and more effective, whether that is programmatic authorities or the parameters or acquisitions or appropriations with respect to CDM?

I know, Mr. Carayiannis, you intimated almost a Phase 5, looking at something to that effect. So I would appreciate your thoughts on that.

Mr. CARAYIANNIS. Well, maybe thinking beyond CDM itself, what it is today and the four phases, one of the concepts we have kicked around and thought about is: How do you extend what the Government is doing around CDM to the community around the Government that is supporting the Government on an on-going basis? If you think about the Government doing more outsourcing on an ongoing basis, you are now more dependent on those resources.

So consequently, I think one thought that the CDM and the committee here should think about is how do we extend some of those principles and guidelines, guidance that you are giving and directives you are giving agencies today around CDM to some of the community that is closest to the Government and helping the Government perform its mission?

Mr. RATCLIFFE. Anyone want in?

Mr. DIMINA. I will agree. I will add to that. I think there is—going back to my testimony today, there is untapped value in CDM today. The data—the intent of the data being collected today is for risk scoring and for asset visibility, and that is great and that is important. That same data could be incredibly valuable for analysts working at DHS, the teams working with EINSTEIN in their mission.

One area where I would suggest additional policy review or oversight is working with DHS to ensure the appropriate rules are in place to access that data for that purpose.

Mr. MOSSBURG. A quick comment on the pace and the speech with which we can continue the journey with CDM. My colleague, Mr. Hodgkins, has mentioned the security clearance issue writ large a couple of times. I think in particular to CDM, when it comes to the contractor community working with DHS to implement for agencies, looking at the reciprocity of security clearances between DHS and the individual agencies, would go a long way to speeding time of delivery on the projects.

Mr. HODGKINS. Mr. Chairman, I also noted several things in my opening statements. The committee can exercise oversight of the appropriations that the agencies take and ensure that they are putting in that line item to fund their CDM activities, where today we do not see that consistently. The committee can look to ensure that appropriate acquisition work force skills are both created and then deployed and that there are sufficient numbers, and then the committee can work both on this program and more broadly across Congress to think about how the Government can acquire commercial capabilities in a more rapid fashion.

We have created a substantial number of Government-unique requirements that have slowed that process down, and those reviews are under way as we speak through various means, but that is a way that we can also look to improve the process the committee can participate in and looking to accelerate.

The cyber work force also we have identified that there is a shortage of those skills, and that is a long-term solution. Then, finally, just oversight of the program, making sure that the different phases are advancing in the way that they are intended and they are advancing in the time frames that are intended.

Mr. RATCLIFFE. I thank you all and I appreciate the panel's indulgence. The Chair now recognizes the gentlelady from Florida, Ms. Demings.

Mrs. DEMINGS. Thank you so much, Mr. Chairman, and also to our Ranking Member and to our witnesses today. Thank you so much for being here.

As we learned from the OPM hack in 2015, agencies need a strong secure system for managing who is authorized to access sensitive data. To address this, CDM Phase 2 calls for the creation of a centralized master user record, among other things, to help agencies manage credentials and privileged access.

This question is for any or all of you. How effective do you think the master user record will be? Are there areas in Phase 2 where it is currently—and how it is currently designed where it falls short?

Mr. MOSSBURG. I will take the first. I do think that the Phase 2, the credential management and the privilege management aspects of Phase 2 are very effective, have the potential to be very effective, not only in the creation of the master user record, but in the policy enforcement of having both the credentials that you and I are used to and a user ID and login, something that we know to access a system, but also a physical asset that we have and a PIV card, or a little ID card. The combination of both will go a long way to preventing the situations like we had with OPM or things that you are familiar with in the private sector, like the Target breach last year.

Mrs. DEMINGS. Others?

Mr. DIMINA. I agree with Mr. Mossburg. The only footnote I will add to that is, it is my understanding that the identity data is key and having information on user behavior is important. I think the challenge there is bringing it all together.

My understanding is the identity data is not currently feeding into dashboard or being correlated with the existing CDM data, and the real power of this program is the ability to do analytics on this data. If that data is not brought together and analytics has not happened, it is a missed opportunity.

Mr. CARAYIANNIS. If I could add, data is key to everything here, so that master user record, the concept of being able to obtain data from not only one agency, but all agencies, being able to access that, bring all that together and associate that to an individual, it is key. So the concept of, you know, if I have very little data, then we are going to have a challenge being able to relate all that to a record, so that is critical in terms of the aggregation of that information to be able to leverage it.

Mrs. DEMINGS. Anyone else want to speak on it? OK, thank you. Also, for any or all of you, from your perspective, what examples do you believe already exist that you feel best demonstrates the value of CDM?

Mr. CARAYIANNIS. I will take that one first. So, thank you, Congresswoman. There was a recent example during the last WannaCry event that occurred where some of the agencies who have been making good progress leveraging and accessing, bringing data together, as a part of CDM was able to leverage that data quickly, do a report on all the information that they had of what systems would potentially be impacted by it and be able to quickly put an action plan in place to address that, and therefore, you know, not have to deal with a very painful experience.

So it was—the good news is, in a very immediate way, while everything is not deployed immediately across the board—we have not gone through all the phases, where are we seeing some agencies get benefit from this by DHS directive, and I think there will be a lot more of that to come as the program continues to build and roll out.

Mrs. DEMINGS. That is great.

Mr. DIMINA. I will add to that. As I mentioned in my testimony, during Phase 1 deployments, there are several agencies that discovered they had additional end-points than they were aware of. So in one perspective, that can be looked at as a challenge. I see it as a positive. I see it as a success story.

The first part of an effective cyber strategy is understanding your footprint and understanding your security posture. That information and that intelligence is a success story and step forward for those agencies in being able to appropriately defend their assets.

Mrs. DEMINGS. That is great. Others? Mr. Mossburg.

Mr. MOSSBURG. I agree wholeheartedly with those two. I will take it from a slightly different angle. I think one of the biggest successes that the CDM program has demonstrated is an incorporation of lessons learned. After going through Phase 1 and Phase 2, DHS and their partners at GSA and Fedsim changed the approach of the program to—in what is now called Defend to accommodate a couple of things.

One very important one was an expanded access to the latest and greatest from industry, in particular with software products, by changing the way those software products could be procured by the agency through the integrator. So it enables greater access to that.

The second was an expansion of the period of performance with the individual projects that will be executed in Phase 3 and Phase 4. What is important about that is, as you have a longer relationship between integrator and agency to deploy the solution, you have greater re-use of the staff from a security clearance standpoint than you had previously. So it gets past some of those obstacles from a pace standpoint around the security clearance.

Mrs. DEMINGS. Thank you. Mr. Hodgkins.

Mr. HODGKINS. I would just add that the program—one of the things that we would see as success is that it is something that can be applied in a relatively uniform fashion across the Government. It is not common to find consistent uniformity for Government requirements in contracting or in plans and protection programs of this nature, so it is a success that this is being rolled out in a consistent, uniform fashion. We have a repeatable activity and a repeatable successes, and measurable, repeatable conclusions that we can draw across agencies.

Mrs. DEMINGS. Thank you. Mr. Chairman, I yield back.

Mr. RATCLIFFE. Thank the gentlelady. The Chair now recognizes the gentleman from Nebraska, Mr. Bacon.

Mr. BACON. Thank you, Mr. Chairman. It is my first time in the committee, so it is good to be part of the subcommittee. It is an honor.

Mr. RATCLIFFE. We are glad to have you.

Mr. BACON. I am a retired 30-year Air Force guy with signals intelligence, and worked a little bit in cyber. One thing I took away from that is we have some of the best cyber capabilities in the world, particularly in the intelligence and the offensive side, but we also had the most vulnerabilities, and I—which you are working that part of it. So thank you for what you are doing.

I heard one of our senior generals say once that we have the biggest rocks, but we also live in the largest glass house when it comes to cyber. So it is a two-edged sword there, right?

Mr. Mossburg, I know you talked a little bit about hygiene or the right cyber hygiene. Could you just talk a little more succinctly, what does that really mean? Where are we at in getting to that proper hygiene?

Mr. MOSSBURG. Sir, I think—and I first referenced it with regard to Phase 1 and the focus on what is on individual networks, and after creating a master device record, an inventory of the assets that exist on the network, a rigorous, constant patching of that software and maintaining the proper configuration is that hygiene.

So we are well into Phase 1, but as I think in early responses, not complete. We do not have that complete inventory yet. But you heard some of the responses here a second ago, with even some of the more recent issues and attacks that we have encountered from WannaCry to some of the recent hardware attacks, our agencies were better prepared because of the—one, the patching that was occurring, the hygiene that was occurring on the devices that had been identified, but also the data that had been collected for even when those devices were not yet being patched or having the proper hygiene applied to them, we at least knew about them, and then the agencies could prioritize their reaction to addressing them and prevent those attacks from causing harm.

Mr. BACON. You are having to do that with all 24 Federal agencies?

Mr. MOSSBURG. Yes, that—all 24 will roll through the Phase 1.

Mr. BACON. Do you have—is the software that you are using, is it the same for all 24? Because I think that would be pretty challenging.

Mr. MOSSBURG. Well, and I think the goal of the CDM program is to have a common approach in these. Quite honestly, CGI is engaged in Phase 2 in the credential management. I would defer to the vendors that are rolling out Phase 1 on the specifics there.

Mr. CARAYIANNIS. I can make a comment about that, Congressman Bacon. At the end of the day, one of the challenges for a lot of the primes, taking the dashboard, deploying it within respective agencies, but to your question, lots of different technologies that will be used by a lot of different agencies. So I think that was one of the complicated elements of what CDM was trying to tackle was leveraging what was already out there, augmenting what was there, and putting into best practice and use of those to deal with the master user record, being able to populate it, have accurate information there. So that is been a big challenge I think for a lot of the prime contractors.

Mr. BACON. Some of these countries are so advanced in this area, it just takes one device that we have not had the patch for to find a vulnerability on, would you agree with that statement?

Mr. CARAYIANNIS. Yes, sir, I would.

Mr. BACON. Mr. Carayiannis, what is the Federal enterprise— where is the Federal enterprise in developing their CDM dashboards from your perspective? Are the barriers to fully implementing and using the dashboard technical, or is it administrative?

Mr. CARAYIANNIS. I would basically say that I think it is a combination of the two, so we have worked very hard to stay as close that we can with DHS, with the dashboard prime, as well as the prime contractors working within the agencies. We are learning a lot of what people need the dashboard to be able to do at the agency level, as well as the Federal level. We have been augmenting our software on an on-going basis. We have a release schedule at least twice a year. The idea around that is to continue to add additional components, upgrades, enhancements to our software to enable them to progress and to do more work, the work that they need to do to drive CDM to success.

Mr. BACON. I appreciate your challenge. I come from the Air Force. We tried to do a dashboard. That was hard enough for the Air Force, because you have different major commands underneath it, airlift, fighter, space. But those dashboards you are building is going to be a one-size-fits-all for all 24 agencies.

Mr. CARAYIANNIS. So the current architected approach—and I think it is the right one—I made that comment in my opening remarks—one of the key elements of this is having consistency from a dashboard tool across the entire agency-level dashboards and at the Federal level. Having consistency, having DHS maintain that consistent approach ensures that you are seeing similar information types, risk scores, et cetera, rolling up to the agency and to the Federal level.

If you did not do that, you have everybody doing something slightly different, to your very point about within the DOD environment, you know, you start seeing a lot of apples and oranges and lots of different variations. So consistency is paramount, in our judgment, from a dashboard perspective, to a CDM program success.

Mr. BACON. I just think with all the different missions, that is a challenge, because everybody has a different mission area and different unique requirements. But yet I understand you have got to standardize if you want to be able to defend the system better, so I had some more questions, but my time is out. Thank you for your expertise and thank you for your service.

Mr. CARAYIANNIS. Thank you, sir.

Mr. RATCLIFFE. Thank the gentleman. Chair now recognizes the gentleman from Rhode Island, Mr. Langevin.

Mr. LANGEVIN. Thank you, Mr. Chairman. I want to thank all of our witnesses for your participation, testimony here today.

Mr. Hodgkins, if I could start with you, obviously, this is a very important topic and appreciate all the contributions you have made to this discussion. But, Mr. Hodgkins, the administration has recently released the report to the president on Federal IT modernization that pushes strongly toward greater adoption of cloud-based applications and services.

Now, CDM has traditionally been focused on identifying and protecting Federal assets within our Federal networks. As Federal assets are deployed in cloud architectures, how well is CDM positioned for this new paradigm? How does the program need to change to ensure it continues to be effective?

Mr. HODGKINS. Well, as I noted in my testimony, Mr. Langevin, cloud deployment of Federal assets was not really a major focus of CDM when it was first formulated and put together. So that is an element that as we—and as I noted about the question on evolution, as those new technologies come into play, as those new efficiencies are identified and the Government adopts those, CDM will need to evolve to address the new risks that might occur because we are moving in different directions with new capabilities.

Mr. LANGEVIN. OK. As a follow-up, are certain CDM phases more or less effective in protecting cloud assets? I certainly would welcome comment from some of the other witnesses on the next question. Does DHS's ability to maintain situational awareness change with respect to cloud solutions?

Mr. HODGKINS. On your first question, sir, the effort to identify the users should be something that can be transferred over when those activities move to the cloud so that you should still have the same type of identification and authentication capabilities, and those should be reusable, if you will. I am not aware that the others are positioned or directly thinking that the vendors at the table may be able to more directly answer that question for you.

Mr. CARAYIANNIS. I was going to make a comment about that, Congressman. So at the end of the day, I made some comments earlier about this universe of contractors or support elements in and around the Government, so if you think about the cloud environment itself, you have organizations that are providing Federally-certified cloud environments, which is a good thing. But I do think that some of the underlying principles and elements of what CDM is should be driven out more broadly to some of those suppliers so they are inheriting some of the inherent capabilities of and underlying tenets of what CDM is trying to do for the Government itself.

Mr. DIMINA. So I will add to that. I think there has been some progress with regards to how we secure the cloud, how do we monitor cloud, and this is where FedRAMP comes into play. I think DHS is looking at that. Cloud has been with us for some time, and it is not going anywhere. So I think that is a problem that is going to be solved.

I think the bigger challenge is, what is going to happen as we move into the internet of things, where every device is connected? How do we secure and monitor mobile devices as we move and solve the human capital gaps we have in our work force and have more people work remotely? How do we deal with the changes and disruptions that are occurring from things such as containerization, and when traditional data centers do not exist anywhere, and where we are in a server-less environment?

So I think those are the bigger challenges ahead. Cloud is certainly important, will be the mechanism for delivery of a lot of these technologies, but those are the ones that if you look longer term, 1 to 3 years out, that will need some proper planning. I think the most important piece here, if you look at the future CDM, is that careful and thoughtful planning has to go into the design decisions made today, because the worst possible outcome would be if a decision made now would prevent the use of some future yet-to-be-released cybersecurity technology or information technology asset. I think some of the delays in Phase 1 were a result of that heavy lift of a lot of those design decisions that had to happen, and we are seeing phases hopefully accelerate now as some of that design work is complete.

Mr. LANGEVIN. Well, this is a good follow-up, good segue into my next question. While CDM now provides a method to streamline acquisition of cybersecurity tools across agencies, it is still incumbent upon each agency to define and execute a risk management strategy and process. How are individual agencies utilizing the tools provided by CDM to create an overall risk management strategy and prioritize their acquisition of cybersecurity tools? Have you observed any changes or improvements since CDM has been implemented? Mr. Hodgkins, if we can maybe start with you.

Mr. HODGKINS. Well, I think the answer to your last question is, yes, there have been improvements since CDM has been deployed. I think that agencies are required to make a different set of assessments and determine their risks more effectively, and CDM is deploying toolsets that helps them try to address and protect against those risks and threats.

I believe that there is obviously room to grow, and I think that agencies can always do a better job of assessing their risks. But we are seeing improvement, and CDM is one of the factors that is contributing to that improvement and their ability to identify those risks and trying to position themselves to protect or defend against it.

Mr. LANGEVIN. OK.

Mr. MOSSBURG. I would just briefly say I agree that we have seen the results since the beginning of the CDM program, but I think it is with the Defend portion that is recently and currently under way where we have got the streamlined acquisition process for the tools where we have the potential to see the greatest benefit for individual agencies to get quicker access to the tools that are specific to their agencies and also as technology evolves with the threats, take advantage in a more—in a quicker fashion some of the latest technology.

Mr. LANGEVIN. Very good. Thank you. Mr. Chairman, I have some additional questions I will submit for the record. If I could have our witnesses respond to them, that would be helpful. Thank you all very much. With that, I will yield back the balance of my time.

Mr. RATCLIFFE. Thank the gentleman. The Chair now recognizes the gentlelady from Texas, Ms. Jackson Lee, for 5 minutes.

Ms. JACKSON LEE. Thank you, Mr. Chairman. Thank you to the Ranking Member, Ranking Member Richmond. This is an important hearing. In fact, the constant oversight of our cybersecurity system is really crucial for the defense of this Nation and, as well, the important responsibilities that are driven by the cyber system.

I heard the words careful and thoughtful planning, and I think that is clearly the framework in which we should be going forward. I have a series of questions, but the thoughtful and careful planning causes me to want to pose a question to you. Even as I know that the Continuous Diagnostics and Mitigation program deals with the attempt to ensure that the Federal network is healthy, but it is the constant changing system—and there are many parts of it that are impacted by the human element.

So just take—you are obviously in the private sector. You know that we are querying about the incident that occurred in Hawaii. Certainly it was a cyber system of sort. Would you speculate on the—what might have been needed, how that translates into what good the system that we are dealing with is trying to do? We are obviously—all of us are paying attention in terms of the massive investigation that is going forward, not only State, but I certainly believe a full Federal investigation should occur, because we have a very important role in the network that States have, as well.

So would you take a moment to comment on how that could have happened and how in the instance of our system it is intended to avoid that? Who wants to start first?

Mr. HODGKINS. I will answer, Ms. Jackson Lee. Thank you for the question. The only commonality that comes to mind based on the reporting that I have seen is human error. Human error is still one of the primary drivers for cyber vulnerabilities, whatever system you are looking at, and so we have to continue to address that with additional training, additional acquisition of more skills, bringing in more people with those skills, and make sure that we try to diminish the opportunity to human error to occur.

Ms. JACKSON LEE. Gentlemen, please.

Mr. CARAYIANNIS. Congresswoman Lee, as I think about your question, I think quite a bit about what CDM is trying to do, which is to automate as many processes as possible and try to take the human factor out of the situational analysis around assets, vulnerabilities, configurations, whatever the case may be. So to the extent that if you try to relate one of the other, yes, the incident as it was reported in the paper, it looks like it was a human error. I think there will always be a human element to what goes on. But CDM is itself—to relate it back which I think was the premise of your question—relate it back to what CDM is about, by taking more control from an automated perspective of your environments, and being able to do something in a very automated way, I think you start to minimize the impact that the human element might have.

Ms. JACKSON LEE. Yes. Thank you.

Mr. MOSSBURG. I will take a slightly different—sorry about that.

Mr. DIMINA. Go ahead.

Mr. MOSSBURG. Slightly different angle. I think another part of the CDM program overall scope will be remediation when an issue occurs. There will always be human elements that factor—as you mentioned, that will come into play, and there will always be that cause. We will continually be adapting to situations such as this.

Our ability to remediate or mitigate when an issue does occur and then put processes in place to prevent it from occurring again and learn those lessons are as crucial as the automation and processes that we can implement.

Mr. DIMINA. So I am not an expert on the incident that happened, but I think a perspective I can give you that might help is what is going on in private sector to deal with the shortages in the human workers and skills and resources and training that has been discussed today.

There is two trends that are under way. The private sector is certainly doubling down its investment in software approaches to these problems. Two of those trends are occurring on—so one I mentioned earlier today about automation orchestration. How do we add as much automation and adaptive capabilities to the system so we are not so dependent on humans? CDM certainly could benefit from that.

On the second trend is the adoption of technologies such as machine learning and data analytics to understand—to help us as practitioners filter through the noise, so that only the important signals get through and our human time is spent more efficiently so that there is less burden on our human resources and less likely of an accident or an incident. These technologies are all receiving major investments in the private sector and will continue to in the near future.

Ms. JACKSON LEE. It is clearly important because of the large percentage of the infrastructure that is in the private sector. Let me quickly ask this question, if I might. CDM will be the first Government-wide effort to centralize the assessment of the cyber health of the Federal computer system. As we well know, it is massive, it is massive, more massive than Hawaii, more massive than another State or the collective States. It is the Federal Government impacting so much.

How well-prepared do you think we are to correctly interpret the information that we will be receiving? Obviously, there is a human element there in receiving and interpreting that information.

Mr. DIMINA. So thank you for that question. I think it is a very important question, and it centers around the theme of my testimony today. CDM provides us a visibility of assets within Government perimeters. What is going on inside the network?

There are additional programs out there such as the Einstein program that provides visibility into what is coming in and out of the network, that perimeter viewpoint. Both of these programs satisfy a critical and necessary need, but today there is no integration between the data of these programs.

So I think to your question is: How do we increase the value we are getting from these investments? One of the ways is by allowing DHS and agencies to benefit from tools such as data analytics to fuse some of the information that they are getting from two programs to more effectively enable the mission to hunt for bad actors and identify the techniques and tactics that are used by these actors.

Ms. JACKSON LEE. I think it is a roadmap that we need to follow. If I could just—Mr. Chairman, indulge me for Mr. Hodgkins, a follow-up question that Mr. Richmond asked, let me combine a question here. Defending against cyber threats is an ever-changing landscape. Can CDM adjust to the rapid changes in technology and applications?

The question I want to follow up, Mr. Hodgkins and Mr. Richmond, is by teaching our youngsters code, as you well know, there is a—you may know, there is an effort to teach code in minority communities, to increase the opportunity. Is that an element of providing for the work force? Is that a productive use as it relates to this kind of work? But the first question is, are we able to adjust to the rapid changes in technology and applications? Then, is training in code productive?

Mr. HODGKINS. Thank you for the question. To your first question, yes, I think the program—it does have the ability to evolve and to position itself as technologies move forward. We have talked about some of that and my counterparts have also shared some elements of that, so I think that the system and the processes that are being put in place—and as we move into Phase 3 and Phase 4, in contract for those, we continue to re-evaluate what does the environment look like, what are the threats, the new threats that perhaps did not exist when we were contracting for Phase 1, how do we incorporate those capabilities? How do we move forward? So the processes that are put in place to implement through phases CDM will continue to evolve and help the program evolve, as well.

Our industry has been very strongly supportive—in answer to your second question—of a variety of programs to try and increase the level of interest in STEM activities across the board, and coding in particular. It is essential that we try and get to students early on. There is multitudes of research that have been shown that getting to students early on and securing their interests before other factors come into play and detract their—distract them, if you will, from taking a STEM-type career path or course path is important, and coding is an element that seems to attract a lot of attention and get a lot of attention of a lot of younger people who grew up in a computer world as a way that they can interact and build a successful career. So we have been supportive and will continue to be supportive of that.

Ms. JACKSON LEE. Thank you very much, Mr. Chairman. I too have additional questions that I would like to submit for the record. Thank you very much to all the witnesses. Thank you for your testimony. I yield back.

Mr. RATCLIFFE. Thank the gentlelady. That concludes our hearing today. I thank the witnesses for your valuable testimony and your insights today. I thank the Members for their questions. As indicated, some Members of the committee have additional questions for the witnesses, and we will ask you all to respond to those in writing.

Pursuant to committee rule VII(D), the hearing record will remain open for a period of 10 days. Without objection, the subcommittee stands adjourned.

[Whereupon, at 3:31 p.m., the subcommittee was adjourned.]

○